MORE HELP!

For Teachers of Young Children

*To you and the other selfless people who dedicate
their lives to the care of young children and their families*

MORE HELP!

For Teachers of Young Children

Gwen Snyder Kaltman

99 Tips
to Promote
INTELLECTUAL
DEVELOPMENT
and
CREATIVITY

CORWIN PRESS
A SAGE Publications Company
Thousand Oaks, California

For information:

Corwin Press
A Sage Publications Company
2455 Teller Road
Thousand Oaks, California 91320
www.corwinpress.com

Sage Publications Ltd
1 Oliver's Yard
55 City Road
London EC1Y 1SP
United Kingdom

Sage Publications India Pvt. Ltd.
B-42, Panchsheel Enclave
Post Box 4109
New Delhi 110 017 India

Printed in the United States of America on acid-free paper

Library of Congress Cataloging-in-Publication Data

Kaltman, Gwen Snyder.
More help!: for teachers of young children: 99 tips to promote intellectual development and creativity / Gwen Snyder Kaltman.
    p. cm.
Includes bibliographical references and index.
ISBN 1–4129–2444–8 (cloth)—ISBN 11–4129–2445–6 (pbk.)
   1. Education, Preschool. 2. Child development. 3. Teaching—Aids and devices—Education (Preschool) 4. Preschool teachers—Training of. I. Title. e.
LB1140.2.K315 2006
372.21—dc22

                              2005010619

05 06 07 08 10   9 8 7 6 5   4 3 2 1

Acquisitions editor:	Stacy Wagner
Production editor:	Sanford Robinson
Copy editor:	Kristin Bergstad
Typesetter:	C&M Digitals (P) Ltd.
Cover designer:	Rose Storey

Contents

Preface

The Australian Aborigines have the longest continuous living culture on the planet. They have no written language. For over 50,000 years, knowledge has been passed from generation to generation by elders who tell stories as a way of entertaining and, more important, educating their people on proper behavior and customs. Wally of the Anangu people told me that an elder will often create a story using mischievous spirits called Mimis to tactfully get across a message. Following in the tradition of the Aborigines and anyone else who has ever told the story of The Three Little Pigs, I too use stories to both entertain and enlighten. My stories are told to help teachers and parents better understand young children, how to interact with them, and how to teach them.

I hope you find the stories so interesting and entertaining that you keep turning the pages because you just can't wait to see the next story. I'd like to suggest that when you are done reading the book you do not put it away on a shelf. Instead, choose a topic that you are comfortable with and reread that chapter. As you do, take the time to think and reflect. How does the material apply to you in your circumstances? What could you try, what could you improve on, how could you modify some of the ideas to fit your particular situation?

Use this book as your own personal mentor. To help you do this, I have included a resource: Creating Your Own Plan for Improvement. Every year your skills and understanding will increase, and your experiences will influence you to see things in a different light. I hope you will use the chapters in this book as mini workshops and refer to them over and over again during the course of your career. My expectations are high; please don't let them frustrate you. Instead, let them inspire you to soar to greater heights.

While what I have written comes from many years of experience in the preschool classroom, my advice is based on established theories and research on child development and learning by psychologists and educators such as Bruner, Dewey, Elkind, Froebel, Piaget, and Vygotsky. The material in this book is equally applicable for both parents and teachers. We are after all on the same team.

I cannot answer all of the questions you may have or predict the problems you will face in the future. I can only offer some of the principles that have guided me over the years. Try to empower young children and give them the time and freedom to explore a rich, safe environment. Recognize that play for the child is not a diversion, but an important way to learn about the world. Understand and respect the children's interests and developmental level. If we are sensitive and observant, they will show us the way.

This book focuses on promoting intellectual development and creativity. I have also written a companion volume, *Help! For Teachers of Young Children,* that addresses the equally important subjects of developing children's social skills and creating positive teacher-family relationships.

Nuts and Bolts

Each chapter in this book contains a brief introduction followed by a number of stories. After each story, I provide help and questions for you to ask yourself. At the end of each chapter is a section called "Try This" that contains a few suggestions for you to try. I hope these will inspire you to think of many more things you can do with children.

Child care provider, care giver, early childhood specialist, preschool teacher, and educarer are just some of the terms frequently used to describe people who work with young children. To keep things simple I use the term *teacher* throughout this book. I use the terms *center* and *school* interchangeably rather than differentiating between them. Finally, to avoid the grammatical awkwardness of "he or she," I use one gender or the other when referring to children. I chose to use the pronoun *she* when referring to a teacher or director because the majority of them are females. My apologies for this slight to the dedicated and much valued men who also work with young children.

In all instances the names have been changed to protect the innocent, the guilty, and me from a lot of phone calls.

My mother taught me a simple philosophy of life. I can still hear her saying, "Don't just take, you should also give back; lend a helping hand to the next guy." I hope you think this book is a helping hand.

Acknowledgments

Choose a job you love and you will never have to work a day in your life.

—Confucius

I had not planned to spend my life working with young children, but the faculty of the University of Maryland introduced me to the wonderful world of early childhood education and from then on I was hooked. I consider myself incredibly lucky to have been taught by such outstanding leaders in the field as James L. Hymes, Jr., Sarah Lou Leeper, Lillian Willse Brown, and Joan Moyer.

Jackie Hill welcomed this girl from Brooklyn to Tennessee and gave me the opportunity to teach at Chattanooga State. I also want to express my appreciation to all of the directors, teachers, students, and families I have worked with through the years.

I owe a great deal to my friends and colleagues, Nora Callahan, Arlene Friedland, Cindy Goodman, Paula Ott, Jo Robbins, and especially Judy Zimmerman, who took the time to read an early draft of the manuscript. They gave me the benefit of their experience and wise council.

I am indebted to Faye Zucker, the executive editor of Corwin Press, for her support. The staff at Corwin Press has worked hard to bring this project to fruition. Their efforts, especially those of Kristin Bergstad, are gratefully acknowledged. Stacy Wagner has been a staunch advocate from the start. Her suggestions and help with the manuscript are deeply appreciated. I could not have wished for a better editor.

Last but not least I want to thank my husband Al and my sons Blaine and Mylan. Their advice and encouragement were truly invaluable.

Corwin Press acknowledges the important contributions of the following reviewers:

Gloria Hearn
Educational Consultant
Hearn & Hearn Consultants
Pineville, LA

S. Jackie Hill
Associate Professor & Early
    Childhood Education
    Program Coordinator
Chattanooga State Technical
Community College, TN

Ruth R. Kennedy
Assistant Professor
Bloomsburg University of
Pennsylvania

Kathleen McGinn
Director of Child Development
    Programs
Colton Joint Unified School
District, CA

Joan Moyer
Professor Emeritus
Arizona State University

Marilyn Segal
Director of Academics, Mailman
Segal Institute for Early
    Childhood Studies
Nova Southeastern University, FL

Joan Franklin Smutny
Director of The Center for Gifted
National-Louis University, IL

Catheryn Weitman
Professor
Barry University, FL

Judy Zimmerman
Executive Director, Mailman Segal
Institute for Early Childhood
    Studies
Nova Southeastern University, FL

About the Author

Gwen Snyder Kaltman has spent more than 25 years working with young children, their parents, and teachers. She is the author of *Help! For Teachers of Young Children: 88 Tips to Develop Children's Social Skills and Create Positive Teacher-Family Relationships.* Kaltman earned her B.S. and M.Ed. in Early Childhood Education from the University of Maryland, and has been a preschool teacher, director, college instructor, and educational trainer in various parts of the country. She has also been a validator for the National Academy of Early Childhood Programs, the accreditation division of the National Association for the Education of Young Children.

Kaltman has worked with young children in Connecticut, Delaware, Georgia, Maryland, Massachusetts, New York, Tennessee, and Virginia. She has trained teachers working in Head Start programs in Chattanooga, Tennessee, and rural Georgia and in child care centers and preschools in the suburbs of New York City and Washington, D.C. She has observed preschool classes in such diverse places as China, Easter Island, Greenland, India, Malta, Mongolia, Tibet, Tanzania, Venezuela, and native villages above the Arctic Circle and along the Amazon and Sepik rivers.

Born and raised in the Bedford Stuyvesant section of Brooklyn, New York, she has been married for over 30 years. While it is true that her gray hairs started growing when she was in high school, she attributes most of them to her two sons.

Introduction: Preparing for Life Through Play

When we think about play for adults we talk about playing ball, cards, chess, computer games, and board games like Scrabble and Monopoly. The play usually requires some level of skill. Play can be very challenging, and many adults make a considerable living "playing" professional sports. By comparison, when we want to indicate that adults are doing nothing we usually say they are chilling out or goofing off.

When associated with young children, the word *play* seems to imply very little of value. Many think of it as the child's way of just chilling out. Nothing could be further from the truth. A child at play is as active and mentally engaged as a quarterback in the last moments of a Super Bowl game. I wish there were another more important-sounding word or term for a child's play—such as *explorientation, life readiness,* or *extreme reality quest*—to give it the importance it deserves.

In almost every nature film I have seen about lions or any other animal there is sure to be an entertaining scene of young cubs playing. The narrator usually tells us that while this appears to be just play, the cubs are actually honing skills they will need as adults. They are, in fact, preparing to grow up. For young children, exactly the same thing is going on. Play is a natural part of a child's preparation to grow up. Through play a child explores materials and ideas about everything in life. Instead of learning to hunt and kill as a lioness cub must do, children start to think about very basic issues. Common subjects of play are good guys and bad guys, power and weakness, real and pretend, speed and safety, and human relationships. In many instances, children will actually think aloud as they grapple with these important topics.

When a child runs around on the playground as a superhero, he is not just playing. He is actively and seriously thinking and wrestling with important issues about humankind, and this helps him prepare for his role in society as an adult. Similarly, when a child builds a pretend road with blocks and then races a car around it she is busy exploring ideas and concepts. She may be thinking about road construction, how things go together (various shapes of blocks), inclines and curves. When she drives the toy car she could be thinking about speed, accidents, safety, the role of the police, how Dad drives, and how she will drive one day.

The natural need and importance of play for the young child cannot be overemphasized. Everything that a child does that is not adult directed is play. It is the most important part of a young child's education. Regardless of language, culture, or economic status, young children play. You will find children playing in the snow of the Arctic, the mud of the Amazon rainforest, the sands of the Sahara desert, the grasslands of Mongolia, the creeks of Louisiana, the mountains of Colorado, and the streets of Detroit, Los Angeles, and New York. Play is truly a universal experience.

You should value play for the necessary part of human development that it represents, and then actively encourage and facilitate it as a part of your program. The way to do this is to provide varied materials, lots of free time for exploration, and on occasion suggestions and guidance toward new subjects and materials for the children to explore and think about. Some of the best learning occurs when children are dealing with materials, having experiences, and discovering ideas and forming concepts for themselves. Play should be an integral part of everything you plan to teach. It is fundamental to human development, and is the foundation of a good early childhood program.

> *Play is the way the child learns what no one can teach him. It is the way he explores and orients himself to the actual world of space and time, of things, animals, structures, and people. . . . Play is a child's work.*
>
> *—Lawrence K. Frank*

"What Should We Do Next Week?"

Creating Developmentally Appropriate Lesson Plans and an Environment That Supports Your Curriculum

One of the great pleasures of teaching the young child is that the teacher is often given both the freedom and responsibility for selecting the activities and materials she will use to meet the goals of the curriculum. I have seen lesson plans on everything from Apples to Zoos. A teacher can choose to focus on anything in the world, including the kitchen sink. Of course, the great challenge is to select activities and materials that are relevant to the world of young children. Let the young child's interests be your guide.

Whatever you choose to focus on, you should enjoy the subject matter. Children are very perceptive, and if you are not interested in a subject, that will be communicated. Remember that young children often learn more than just the facts we think we are teaching them. In the final analysis, the most important lesson we can teach is the pleasure that comes from learning.

Having children recite facts or parrot information told to them by an adult is counterproductive. There is a danger that what the children are really learning is that education is a meaningless, boring exercise of memorizing facts to please an adult. Lengthy talks by teachers and focusing on subjects not in the child's immediate world are best saved for later years.

Before writing any lesson plans you need to take the time to get to know the children. Observe them carefully and try to assess what they are capable of doing. We know that trying to teach a child to walk before he can crawl is a waste of time and would only frustrate the child. It is just as futile and frustrating to try to teach academic subjects before a child is developmentally ready.

No two children are identical. In order to be responsive to different learning styles and developmental levels we need to provide many different types of activities with varying degrees of complexity. By doing this we help children grow and develop to their full potential, without overwhelming any individual child.

For convenience, the remaining chapters in this book are organized by content areas; however, keep in mind that it really is impossible to compartmentalize learning because all learning is integrated. For example, the simple cooking experience of making cupcakes involves reading (a recipe), mathematics (counting and measuring ingredients), and science (observing the effect of heat on the liquid batter).

I cannot overemphasize how important it is for you to design developmentally appropriate lesson plans based on the concept that young children learn through play and activity. They need a lot of free time to enjoy hands-on experiences. Children learn and form their own ideas when they can observe and manipulate materials. Most of what they learn in the early years is through their five senses.

The aim of education should be to teach the child to think, not what to think.

—*John Dewey*

1. Plan activities for large and small motor development

LOUNGE CHAIR LIZARD

Mindy was a most agreeable four-year-old. She got along very well with the adults and all the children. She had a wonderful smiley face. Being pleasantly plump, her eyes would practically disappear into her full cheeks whenever she smiled. One warm afternoon, Mindy was sitting on the grass in the shade of a tree. This was one of her favorite spots and activities (or inactivity) when on the playground. I was delighted with her unusual request for a turn on the tricycle.

When it was Mindy's turn she got up and slowly walked over to the tricycle. I had never seen her on a tricycle, and was delighted with the prospect of observing her being physically active. She mounted the tricycle and pedaled it about 10 feet—heading straight for the shaded area under a porch overhang. Once there, she promptly got off the tricycle and carefully positioned it against a wall so that it would not roll. Mindy then proceeded to climb on the seat and sit down backwards. She leaned back and rested her elbows on the handlebars, and in so doing turned the tricycle into a lounge chair! She looked like someone relaxing at the beach.

The staff all chuckled at this surprising turn of events. It certainly was a creative way to use a tricycle.

HELP!

There are many children like Mindy who when left to their own choices, always seem to prefer sedentary activities. This can become a serious problem. A lack of physical activity coupled with a poor diet leads to obesity. Young children need to be active to develop their large muscles. Too often teachers assume that just letting the children go out on the playground for 15–20 minutes a day guarantees that the children's need for large motor development is being met. Clearly this is faulty logic. In addition to providing free time, we need to plan activities that encourage all the children to climb, run, and jump. To encourage large motor development:

- ✯ Set up an obstacle course where children have to go over, under, and through objects
- ✯ Organize relay races
- ✯ Organize a tricycle parade
- ✯ Play ball games
- ✯ Do developmentally appropriate physical exercises
- ✯ Play games like follow the leader

> Do not limit large motor activity to the playground; bring it indoors as well. When doing music, include opportunities for activities such as jumping, running, and crawling.

Small motor control and eye-hand coordination are also important elements of a child's physical development. Without them a child cannot learn to read and write. Lesson plans should always include activities that encourage small motor development such as:

- ✯ Doing puzzles
- ✯ Playing with pegs
- ✯ Painting with Q-tips
- ✯ Using play dough
- ✯ Playing with small blocks
- ✯ Turning the pages of a book
- ✯ Threading items such as beads on a string
- ✯ Using crayons
- ✯ Using scissors or tearing paper
- ✯ Using paste

ASK YOURSELF:

Do your lesson plans include activities for large muscle development, small motor control, and eye-hand coordination?

2. Role model curiosity and enthusiasm

CURIOSITY DOES NOT KILL THE CAT

I often think about what makes some people interested in everything while others seem to be bored with life. I have been lucky to share my life with a guy who is curious about everything. We have traveled to see many of the wonders of the world, from Uluru (Ayers Rock) in Australia to the world's largest ball of twine in Branson, Missouri. His curiosity is not limited to a favorite subject. Art, music, ancient civilizations, geology, and animal life all hold a fascination for him.

After many years of close and careful observation, I have come to believe that it is just the sheer satisfaction of learning something new that he finds rewarding. With each new bit of knowledge there is another door opened on something else to find out about.

HELP!

With everything we do, we should try to foster enthusiasm and curiosity. Be a good role model by saying such things as, "Wow, this is exciting. This is really interesting; I want to know more about this. I feel good because I have learned something that I didn't know before." We can role model curiosity and enthusiasm by doing such things as:

✧ Opening up a piano so the children can see how the hammers hit the strings to make sound
✧ Watching a spider spin a web
✧ Looking at a rock collection
✧ Listening to the sound of a tuba
✧ Watching a bird build a nest
✧ Observing a construction site
✧ Mixing different colors
✧ Looking at grass, rocks, or clouds in the sky

We live in a wonderfully fascinating world, and if we present it with a joyful spirit of exploration, we can help children keep their natural curiosity.

Children have never been very good at listening to
their elders, but they have never failed to imitate them.

—*James Baldwin*

ASK YOURSELF:

Do you show enthusiasm and interest in the subjects you present to the children?

3. Select activities and materials that are relevant to the young child

SQUIRRELS VERSUS LEOPARDS

The four-year-old classroom was decorated with a large painting hanging on the wall. The teacher had obviously put a great deal of time and effort into making it. She had painted palm trees, many plants, a monkey, and a leopard. The stories she planned to read were about tropical birds, insects, and creatures that lived in the rainforest.

HELP!

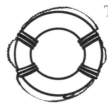

Too many teachers forget that the child's world is the here and now. Topics such as dinosaurs, outer space, the arctic, or the rainforest are poor choices because they are so remote from the immediate world of the young child.

Subjects that the child can explore through observation and/or interaction are best. For example, a squirrel, while not very exotic, is a good choice. Most children will, near their home, on the way to school, or even better yet on the playground, be able to observe a REAL LIVE squirrel—the chances of seeing a monkey or leopard, other than in a zoo, are of course remote. Choose subjects that are relevant to the immediate world of young children, can be explored and observed firsthand, and provide concrete experiential learning opportunities, such as:

- ☆ Apples
- ☆ Balls
- ☆ Seeds
- ☆ Boxes
- ☆ Rocks
- ☆ Pets
- ☆ Tools

Nothing ever becomes real till it is experienced.

—John Keats

ASK YOURSELF:

Do you select activities and materials that are relevant to the child's immediate world and provide concrete experiential learning opportunities?

4. Let the children's interest level determine when it is time to move on to another subject

THERE IS NOTHING SACRED ABOUT A WEEK

One of my favorite subjects was Transportation. I usually talked about trains on Monday, airplanes on Tuesday, trucks on Wednesday, boats on Thursday, and wrapped everything up on Friday. One year, as usual, I had talked about trains on Monday. The children showed great interest. They built train tracks in the block corner, and even lined up chairs in the center of the room to make a pretend passenger train.

On Tuesday, I was presenting material on airplanes. I had a collection of toy airplanes, and made an airstrip with mural paper on the floor in the block corner. During free play Terrell came over to me rather upset. "Where are the trains?" he asked. I said I put them away because today we were talking about airplanes. "But I want to play with the trains," he complained. I was a bit unhappy—I was now moving on to airplanes, and Terrell was trying to relive yesterday.

I had a long commute home and thought about Terrell as I drove. I decided he was definitely right, and I had been missing an important point.

It reminded me of a bus tour that I had taken. We drove around from place to place with hardly enough time to catch our breath. One day here, two days there, half a day somewhere else. After a while you wondered where you were. I felt as though I had seen everything, and at the same time I had seen nothing. How much more satisfying it would have been if I could have lingered long enough to stroll on a street, walk into a supermarket, ride a subway, or go to a local park. The tour guide seemed to have a mission, moving a group of people from point A to point B in the shortest amount of time possible. Now I was doing the same frustrating thing to my students.

I had spent all day Monday getting them interested in trains, and then on Tuesday, when they were ready to explore on their own, I was pulling them in another direction. Were the children going to be introduced to everything but really experience nothing?

HELP!

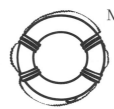

Many teachers plan on studying a different topic every week. They suffer from something I call "one-weekitis." There really is no need to limit ourselves to only five days to explore a topic.

If the children are interested, you can easily spend more than a week on a topic. When given enough time to explore, children can begin to make interesting observations and comparisons of their own. As a result, their play and understanding will be much richer and deeper. Another added benefit is that having gone to the trouble to gather materials on a subject you can now use them for more than just one day or one week. We should not rush things; let the children set the pace. Only when the children show signs of boredom is it time to move on to another topic.

For instance, with trains we can introduce information on:

- ✭ Passenger trains with sleeping compartments and dining cars
- ✭ Subways
- ✭ Commuter trains
- ✭ Boxcars
- ✭ Freight trains

Flight is another very rich topic. We can study:

- ✭ Helicopters
- ✭ Propeller and jet aircraft
- ✭ Passenger and cargo planes
- ✭ Gliders
- ✭ Hot air balloons

Do not limit yourself to preparing lessons that are always topic related. There are many materials, activities, games, songs, stories, and art experiences that have no particular bearing on a topic but are developmentally appropriate and fun.

Be sure there is enough flexibility in the schedule to allow you to focus on events spontaneously, such as a snowstorm, new baby, or other special happenings in the children's lives.

ASK YOURSELF:

Do you spend more than one week on a subject to allow the children time to explore it in depth?

Do you consider the children's interest level before shortening or lengthening the time you spend on any topic?

Do you let topics dominate your choice of activities and materials?

Do you remain flexible so you can respond to the children's interests and take advantage of unplanned-for events such as a snowstorm or a nearby construction project?

Do you allow enough time to do old favorites that are not topic related?

5. Share lesson plans and goals with your staff

WHAT ARE WE TEACHING?

After observing a class for a morning, I asked the teacher, "What are you studying this week?" She responded that they were talking about animals getting ready for winter. I walked over to the assistant teacher and asked the very same question. Her response was "Oh, you know, leaves and things." I then asked the other assistant in the room the same question. She shrugged her shoulders and said, "I don't know." How sad that the other adults in the room did not understand or bother to know what the teacher was trying to accomplish.

HELP!

 It is the lead teacher's responsibility to help all of the adults in her classroom work together as a well-coordinated team. To help establish a team environment, weekly lesson plans need to be discussed before they are implemented. The plans should be more than just a list of activities that show how the children will be kept busy during the week. They should also include goals for the children.

The nice thing about teamwork is that you always have others on your side.

—Margaret Carty

ASK YOURSELF:

Do you try to create a team atmosphere with the other adults in the room?

Do you prepare lesson plans that help them understand what you are trying to teach?

6. Create developmentally appropriate lesson plans that stimulate but do not overwhelm the children

ENTHUSIASM

Mrs. Dizzy, the teacher of the four-year-old class, was the most enthusiastic teacher I have ever met. Bursting with energy, she was a natural-born cheerleader. Every day without fail she would greet the children with compliments and high-five handshakes. She was the kind of person who could exhaust you from just observing her in action.

Her lesson plans for the week were carefully written in detail. It was mid-October and the subject that the children were studying was "Fall Leaves." To add enrichment to her program, she was also studying the alphabet three days a week. For circle time on Tuesday, she planned to do the letter H and bring in several hats to talk about. Wednesday was the letter I, and the discussion topic would be ice. Thursday, the letter J, and she would provide different types of jelly for the children to sample at circle time. In the dramatic play area she had medical equipment for the children to play with.

HELP!

Each one of the lessons Mrs. Dizzy chose was well thought out and developmentally appropriate, but there were just too many lessons on too many subjects. When you added them all up, the total was overwhelming and confusing. We should try to provide a rich environment for the children to explore; however, we must also be able to show some self-control and restraint. Children can be overwhelmed and over-stimulated by their environment. Not every idea we get can be implemented or supervised well. We need to remember the developmental level of the children and make appropriate choices. Don't let your enthusiasm misguide you into making overly ambitious plans that are not realistic or developmentally appropriate. More is not always better.

ASK YOURSELF:

Do you keep in mind the children's developmental level when planning activities for your class?

Do you recognize the difference between a rich environment and one that is so over-stimulating, unfocused, or disorganized that it overwhelms the children?

7. Make plans that are responsive to the children's sense of time

BODY TIME

After my husband meticulously reset all the clocks in our house for daylight savings time, he announced, "We have eighteen clocks in the house." Wow, I thought, that sure sounds like a lot. Yet with all those clocks available and set accurately enough to launch a rocket ship, my dear love is still almost always late for anything we do. I have finally adjusted to the fact that he has his own sense of time.

HELP!

 In most schools teachers have to adhere to a schedule for the use of the playground and when meals will be served. But the need to stay on schedule should be kept in balance with the tempo of the children. Free play may be scheduled to end at 10:30, but if things are going well, and the children are productively engaged, I do not let the clock on the wall dictate to me that things must end. Sometimes this may mean that we have a little less time on the playground, a shorter story, or even a slightly shorter lunchtime. Conversely, if the children are just too stimulated and not settling well into planned activities, I chuck the plans and try something else. We really need to stay responsive to the children's needs. Their body clock is a much better gauge than the clock on the wall.

The children's clock should be respected in structured as well as non-structured situations. When you keep children in a group for too long a time, they will let you know by becoming restless, inattentive, or even starting to misbehave. When thinking about daily plans remember to alternate structured activities (where the adult is in charge) and non-structured ones. Children must have time to explore, make their own choices and decisions. Asking them to stay in a structured group, even if it is small, for too long a time is not developmentally appropriate.

ASK YOURSELF:

Do you keep the class on a regimented schedule or are you flexible and responsive to the children's needs?

Do you alternate structured and nonstructured activities?

8. Let the child decide how long to stay at an activity

QUIT WHILE YOU ARE AHEAD

A student teacher had set up one of the tables to be used during free play with a counting game. It involved spinning a number wheel and then moving a token along a board. When free play began, Zhang, Alicia, and Lori all wanted to play. After a few minutes Lori became restless and lost interest in the activity. She said she was done now and wanted to go play. The student teacher was very disappointed and began to cajole Lori to finish the game she had started. Lori reluctantly agreed and finished the game.

HELP!

The student teacher understandably wanted Lori to finish the game, but did not understand the high cost involved. For several days after that Lori would not go anywhere near the table that had games. Instead of learning about counting, the real lesson that Lori had learned was that she would not be able to leave when she wanted, and therefore it was best to avoid the situation completely.

Too often an adult makes the mistake of wanting to do just one more thing with a child. How many times have we all said, "It will take just a few seconds," when a child was ready to leave an activity but we still had one more important fact or thing to teach. I have found that, as frustrating as it might be at the moment, the best policy is to let THE CHILD decide when she has had enough. By being willing to let them come and go as they choose, you will have better luck getting them to try a game or activity in the future.

> You can't teach much if the child isn't even willing to sit down with you, and the child will be much more willing to sit down IF you are willing to let her leave when she decides it is time to go.

ASK YOURSELF:

Do you allow children to move freely about the classroom and select their own activities?

Do you permit children to decide how much time they will spend at an activity?

9. Help children through transitions by giving them advance notice before changing activities

FAIR WARNING

It is getting near the end of free playtime. A few children are still at the art table, Jeanne has finally been given a turn as the Mommy in housekeeping, and Christopher has just started his turn with the red truck. The teacher rings the bell to signal cleanup time and pandemonium breaks out. Jeanne howls that she wants to be the Mommy, Fran kicks the blocks over in anger, and Christopher throws the red truck that he has been patiently waiting for across the room. It will be tough for the teacher to get cooperation for cleanup.

HELP!

As adults we use many clues to know when an event will be ending. Clocks, body language, or even the sky getting dark at the end of a winter's day all help us do this. Young children really need help easing into transitions. Whether they are getting ready for lunch, naptime, or going home, if they are suddenly told to clean up without any prior warning, it comes as a shock! The simple introduction of an announcement that it is "ALMOST cleanup time, we have another five minutes" helps children learn to adjust. They can get in one last turn or finish up in a hurry whatever it is that they are doing. An additional two-minute warning can be even more helpful.

I remember two young boys who loved playing in the block corner. Whenever I would announce that it was almost cleanup time and this was the last turn at the art table, they would quickly scurry over to the art table. Art was always done in a flurry, but they knew they could squeeze it in at the last minute if they so chose. I was always delighted to welcome them.

ASK YOURSELF:

Do you give children some advance notice prior to a change in activities to help them make a smooth adjustment?

10. Give children the freedom to explore their environment

THEY JUST LIKE TO SIT

My first introduction to a child care center was as a result of a class assignment. I was to visit a center, observe the program, and then write a report based on my observations. I picked a center at random from the phone book and arranged an appointment with the director.

To say this was an eye-opening experience is a gross understatement. The director was busy preparing food and chatted with me while stirring a pot of pasta. When I asked about seeing the two-year-old class, she told me that really wasn't necessary, and tried to talk about the lunch program instead. After being insistent, I was finally permitted to see the toddler class.

Six children were sitting, strapped into high chairs arranged in a semicircle. There were no toys visible anywhere in the room. The teacher was playing a tape of pop music and dancing. I assume she was trying to entertain the children. It really wasn't working. There was a lot of crying and fussing. I asked if the children were about to eat lunch (since they were in high chairs). I was told, "No, they just like to sit."

HELP!

Confining very young children to high chairs, playpens, cribs, swing chairs, or the like for long periods of time is detrimental to their development. Exploration and hands-on experiences are like food for the brain. Using the five senses to explore the environment is vital to a child's development. The ability to see, hear, touch, taste, smell, and hold different objects, move about freely, look at pictures or out of windows is an important part of what the curriculum for the very young child should be.

Gather up safe materials from balls to xylophones for the children to see, touch, and explore. Since the tongue and mouth have the most nerve endings and are the most sensitive, everything that can possibly go in the mouth will. We must ensure that the environment is both safe and clean so we can encourage the children's exploration.

ASK YOURSELF:

Do you provide varied materials and a safe, clean environment for the children to explore?

Do they have the time and freedom to explore or are they almost always under strict control, seated at tables, or engaged in adult-supervised activities?

11. Provide a good physical environment with some privacy zones

AWAY FROM THE MADDENING CROWD

It was three-year-old Jorge's first school experience. While he was no longer crying, he had not yet fully adjusted to the classroom routine. The one activity he did engage in was block building. Frequently he would build the same structure. It resembled a little fort or shelter. He would then fill it up with stuffed animals and a blanket he had brought from home.

HELP!

It is a very long day for most children in child care. No matter what they are doing, they are usually in a group. They are expected to eat, sleep, and even bathroom together. We adults can usually control some part of our work schedules. We can get away for a few moments to be by ourselves and have some time to relax or regroup during a stressful day. It is very important for children to also have a place and the opportunity to get away from the maddening crowd.

A private, quiet nook or zone should be a part of every classroom. A place where the children understand they can go to get away from it all. If space and budget allow, I would include a large stuffed chair to sit in, some pillows and large stuffed animals. There could also be pictures of family members in an album of photos from home. Music and some favorite books would enrich the atmosphere as well.

> Creating a cozy corner is a very worthwhile investment. When children are feeling sad or dealing with rejection or separation problems, it is a very comforting place to go. It is used most often in the beginning of the year, but it should be available all year long.

I'd like to share a few additional thoughts on the subject of room arrangement and the physical environment. We want to provide a safe environment that is designed for the young child. Appropriately sized tables and chairs are important for comfort and safety. Try to arrange the furniture and materials in the classroom so as to create different centers of interest rather than one large open space that can be too stimulating. For example, a reading corner, art area (preferably near a sink), block corner, and a dramatic play area with a large safety (shatterproof) mirror. Store and display equipment and toys in open containers that are within easy reach of the children. Use low shelves and picture labels so the children can identify where things belong.

Ideally the playground should have sunny and shady areas, as well as equipment for different ages and skill levels. A few swings or one climbing structure is really not enough. Try to think about making alternate arrangements for physical activity when children cannot go outdoors because of bad weather.

ASK YOURSELF:

Do you have a cozy corner in your classroom where a child can have some privacy and just get away from it all for a short time or for as long as he needs?

Do you provide a safe, developmentally appropriate environment for young children?

Do you arrange furniture and materials into centers of interest?

Do you store materials in open bins on low shelves so they are easily accessible?

12. Provide hands-on materials

COMPUTERS ALONE ARE NOT ENOUGH

I can clearly recall the first time a computer was used in my preschool classroom. When the children noticed the monitor being carried in, they gathered around the table where it was to be placed. As I fumbled with wires and connections, four of the children placed chairs in front of the table, obviously anticipating a video or TV show. After a few minutes they became bored and drifted off to other activities. I was initially concerned that the computer would be an activity for one child at a time and no social interaction would take place. That concern proved to be half valid. In most situations, one child handled the controls while a group of observers gave advice or just watched the screen.

HELP!

Both computers and computer programs designed for young children have come a very long way since my initial contact with them. While you can usually find a cluster of children gathered around the computer, they are not interacting at the same level of intensity that you would find in the block corner or dramatic play area. Computers are a very nice addition to a classroom, but they should not be purchased at the expense of other more basic materials. Furniture for a housekeeping area, books, puzzles, a generous supply of wooden blocks, toy cars, trucks, people and animal figures are far more important at this age. Young children need the hands-on, interactive experiences that these materials provide.

> Be sure your materials include multicultural, non-gender-bias toys and books.

ASK YOURSELF:

Do you recognize that while computers are important they cannot take the place of hands-on materials for the children to work with?

Do you provide developmentally appropriate programs to use on the computer, if you have one available for the children?

Are there multicultural and non-gender-bias toys and books available?

13. Modify the environment to keep it interesting

VARIETY IS THE SPICE OF LIFE

One of the many joys of working with young children is watching them use materials in fresh and unique ways. One year the block corner was not getting the traffic level that I wanted. Having already gone through props of cars, trains, and animals, I was really pressed for some new way to entice the children to this part of the room. In desperation I decided to add a fabric box along with a collection of little people. The fabric box contained different sizes of scrap cloth, yarn, ribbons, Styrofoam squiggles, scraps of aluminum foil, crepe paper, pie tins, egg cartons, and some other miscellaneous items. During the course of the next few weeks I had some wonderful building and dramatic play to go with it. The following is a list of some of the things the children created and played with:

- ☆ A circus (fabric for tent, ribbons for costumes, string for high wire)
- ☆ An aquarium (the Styrofoam squiggles were the fish)
- ☆ A castle (flags made of crepe paper and ribbons)
- ☆ A tent (square of cloth)
- ☆ A jungle (ribbons and string were snakes)
- ☆ A hospital (all the beds were made with scraps of cloth, ribbons were bandages)
- ☆ A moon station (the egg carton was the passenger rocket ship)
- ☆ A stage for performances (inverted pie tin)
- ☆ A boat (pie tin)

HELP!

We do not do the same story or art activity day after day. We recognize that it would be too boring. We also need to think about our materials and equipment, and how we can add variety to them as well. Try to rotate toys on a regular basis. Do not put out everything you have in September, or you will have some very bored children by January. Put some toys in the closet for a few weeks, then bring them back out and let the children rediscover them.

If other teachers are willing, rotating toys between classes works very nicely as well. Sometimes what seems like a dud in one class becomes a favorite in another. You can never tell with young children.

ASK YOURSELF:

Do you modify the environment and keep it stimulating by moving, adding, or subtracting different materials and equipment?

Do you rotate toys, books, and materials on a regular basis?

14. Display and rotate interesting pictures in your room

A PICTURE GALLERY

One year I used a three-foot-high bulletin board as a room divider to try to give the children playing in the housekeeping area a little more privacy. The divider looked rather barren so I put a few pictures on it to spruce things up. The pictures I had on hand were a group of rabbits, a whale, and a boy with a turtle. This was an immediate hit. Children who did not ordinarily go to the housekeeping area were now visiting to see the new pictures. The children wanted to talk about them.

I decided this was such a good idea that I began collecting and posting pictures. Lightning bolts, fireworks, giant redwood trees, microscopic plants, people hugging, and a chimpanzee playing with a telephone were just some of the pictures that were displayed during the course of the year. The picture gallery became a gathering place where children would get into stimulating conversations—almost like a coffeehouse for four-year-olds.

HELP!

I am an avid believer in the power of pictures. I never sit and look at a magazine without a pair of scissors in my hand. I have found most receptionists in dentist and doctors' offices to be very understanding about my collecting habit. Nature magazines, scientific journals, catalogs, travel brochures, and newspapers are all good sources of pictures. To help preserve the pictures, laminate them or put them in inexpensive protective plastic sheets. You can also put pictures on tables. Cover the picture with clear contact paper to hold it in place.

> Pictures should be rotated frequently.

ASK YOURSELF:

Do you display thought-provoking pictures?

Are the pictures rotated with some regularity?

15. Provide a clean and healthy environment for the children

SOMETHING'S SMELLY

A dear friend, who worked for many years in the early childhood field, was asked by her daughter-in-law to help her select a nursery school. Samantha, her two-year-old, was ready for a group experience. They visited a number of schools looking for the best place. One day, with Samantha in tow, they visited a school that seemed perfect. The large bright rooms were well equipped, there was a lovely playground, and the philosophy of the school on discipline and supportive environment matched theirs. However, they became aware of a problem. As they walked through the infant room, they noticed an unpleasant odor. They continued walking down the hall and went into the toddler room. There they realized the smell was urine. The odor seemed to get worse when they visited the three- and four-year-old classrooms. They were disappointed because they had really liked the school. It was a relief to get some fresh air out on the parking lot. As they drove home, wondering if they would ever find the right school, they again started to smell urine. The mother reached back to check on Samantha, and found her diaper was absolutely saturated. No wonder they had smelled urine everywhere they went!

HELP!

Keeping a classroom clean and providing a healthy environment is a very important part of a teacher's job. We need to wash our hands frequently to cut down on the spread of germs, and keep toys, tables, chairs, and floors clean. Disposing of soiled diapers properly and keeping the bathroom clean is also a very important responsibility. Your sense of smell is a good indicator of the cleanliness of your room; just be sure you know who or what you are smelling.

The children's daily routines—washing hands, eating, brushing teeth, and toileting—provide excellent opportunities to teach good health habits.

ASK YOURSELF:

Do you keep the classroom clean to prevent the spread of germs?

Do you wash your hands frequently?

Do you regularly inspect toys and equipment both in- and out of doors for safety and cleanliness?

Try This

When making lesson plans:
- ☆ Invite aides and assistant teachers to plan activities
- ☆ Ask parents to suggest topics that their children would enjoy exploring
- ☆ Ask children what they are interested in studying

Each year add new activities and materials to your repertoire to avoid becoming stale.

Try studying some unusual subjects such as:
- ☆ Brushes
- ☆ Eggs
- ☆ Luggage
- ☆ Shoes
- ☆ Hair
- ☆ Noses
- ☆ Chairs
- ☆ Kites
- ☆ Hats
- ☆ Fruit
- ☆ Paper
- ☆ Wheels

To facilitate play:
- ☆ Vary materials in block corner, art corner, and dramatic play area with some regularity
- ☆ Arrange room in a new way
- ☆ Ask children for ideas about arranging the room

On the playground use chalk to create paths for children to follow, lines to walk on, areas to jump over, or small circles to step on like stepping stones in a brook. Of course, children will enjoy drawing their own creations.

"Won't You Be My Neighbor?"

Using Social Studies to Help Children Learn About Their Community and to Cherish Diversity

The primary purpose of social studies should be to help the young child develop a positive self-image and the critical thinking skills that are the foundations of good citizenship. Emphasizing the similarities as well as the differences between people helps young children learn to value themselves, each other, their families, and the richness of different cultural heritages. By exploring their school community, neighborhood environment, and the world around them, young children can be taught to develop positive attitudes that celebrate diversity and encourage inclusion. Helping children learn to respect and embrace the wonderful diversity that our society and the world have to offer is essential and should be an integral part of all that we teach.

> We want to raise our children so that they can take a sense of pleasure in both their own heritage and the diversity of others.
>
> —Mister Rogers

16. Create an atmosphere of respect and consideration for others

I'M ME, I'M SPECIAL

Tanya and Jesse were quietly playing in the housekeeping area. They were each tending to their respective dolls. Barbara was wandering about the room aimlessly, and then noticed the activity in the housekeeping area. She approached Tanya and Jesse. Unfortunately, there were only two dolls in the room, and they were both being used. This did not stop Barbara. She grabbed an arm of one of the dolls and tried to yank it away from Tanya. The teacher saw this and went over to stop the tug of war that the poor doll had to endure. Tanya was yelling "It's mine, I had it first." Barbara, in a strong assertive voice, responded, "But I want it, and I'm special."

HELP!

One of the most popular topics studied in preschool is "I'm me, I'm special." Taught carefully, this provides an excellent opportunity for children to develop a positive self-image. However, Barbara's insistence that she should get the doll because she is special illustrates my concern about the possible downside of teaching "I'm me, I'm special" when we should be teaching "I'm me, I'm special, and so are YOU!"

I believe we must temper our lessons of "I'm me, I'm special" by creating an awareness that the child sitting next to you is also special, and is deserving of respect and consideration. We need to be careful that in our enthusiasm to develop confident youngsters with a good self-image, we do not inadvertently create arrogant self-centered children.

> We must help children learn to get along and function in society. It will negatively affect a child to have either an inferiority or superiority complex.

A person is a person, no matter how small.

—Dr. Seuss

ASK YOURSELF:

Do you foster an atmosphere of respect and consideration for other children?

17. Be nonjudgmental and accepting of different families

WHAT'S A FAMILY?

Before a child starts school I invite the parents to bring their child in to the classroom for a visit. When four-year-old Rohit came, he brought along his father and older brother, two uncles, grandmother, and grandfather. Rohit was obviously part of a caring, loving family.

HELP!

 Just as children must learn to crawl before they can walk, they need to learn about themselves before learning about others. After focusing on "I'm me, I'm special" it is only natural to then turn our attention to each child's family. Depending on the culture and circumstances, "family" can mean many different things to different people. Having children talk about their families and the people who care for them is important. In these discussions we can help children appreciate the fact that while each family is different, all are special and caring in their own way.

♦ Remember that a pet is often considered a member of the family.

ASK YOURSELF:

Do you talk about families in a nonjudgmental way?

18. Help children develop positive attitudes toward diversity

WHERE DO YOU SLEEP?

The first school I taught at was housed in a community center building. It had a very large activity area, bathroom, and a small kitchen. The second week of school Laticia asked me, "Where do you sleep?" She had been looking around but could not find my bed. I told her I slept in my bed at home. She smiled and said, "No, you live here." I decided the first trip for the school year would be to my home.

I gave the children a royal tour of my apartment. Points of interest were the pots and pans I used to cook supper, photos of my parents and brother on my desk, my toothbrush, my closet, my toys, and my slippers neatly tucked under my bed. I thought this was such a good experience to help the children see me as a person and not just a teacher that I repeated it every year. No, nothing was ever broken.

HELP!

I think it is always a good idea to offer the children information about yourself. When leading discussions about "I'm me, I'm special," families, or where you live, you should be a contributing but not dominating participant. Visiting the homes of classmates is an excellent way to stimulate discussions of cultural differences. It gives us another opportunity to notice both differences and similarities in a nonjudgmental way.

Different does not mean better or worse, just different. We need to help children learn to recognize similarities and to embrace differences.

> If visits are not practical, try showing pictures or videos. If the school has a video camera, this is a great opportunity to put it to good use.

We all live with the objective of being happy; our lives are all different and yet the same.

—Anne Frank

ASK YOURSELF:

Do you talk about the children's homes?

Do you help children develop a positive view of diversity by noting differences and similarities in a nonjudgmental way?

19. Use music, games, and stories to help children appreciate diversity

NO TRANSLATION NECESSARY

When living in the Washington, D.C., area I felt fortunate to come in contact with people from many different lands and cultures. To tap into this rich resource, I would invite parents to bring in materials to share with the class. We saw beautiful native costumes, learned about customs and children's games, listened to tapes of lullabies in many different languages, and ate some GREAT food. It was tough on my waistline.

One year a Dad from Korea wanted to read his son's favorite story to the class. And he wanted to read it in Korean! My gut reaction was to respond, "Are you crazy, I have enough trouble getting some of these children to pay attention to my stories, and I read in English!" But I controlled myself. It seemed so important to the father that, after some thought, I agreed to his request. I decided the only downside would be an inattentive group of children.

We decided that he would read a page in Korean, and I would then translate it into English. (He provided the translation.) He understood that we might not get to finish the story, as the children might become restless.

It was an amazing experience. This heretofore reserved, quiet man was transformed. He was a terrific storyteller. He kneeled down and whirled his arms about as he described a genie coming out of a bottle, then he jumped up and boldly stood with his arms outstretched as he portrayed a warrior. My English translations were hardly needed at all. I felt as though I was slowing things down by taking the time to translate. The children were absolutely spellbound and understood all that was going on. It was a wonderful experience for all of us.

HELP!

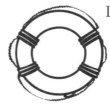
In future years, using the same game plan, I invited people to tell children's stories in Finnish, Dutch, Spanish, Swahili, Chinese, French, German, and Thai. Hearing the rhythm and inflection of another language was an enriching experience.

Sharing traditions and customs from different cultures is a good way to appreciate the diversity in our society and the world. Even if you do not have children in your class from different ethnic backgrounds you still can and should read stories, play games, listen to music, prepare foods, and celebrate holidays of different cultures.

ASK YOURSELF:

Do you help the children in your class appreciate diversity by listening to music, playing games, celebrating holidays, and reading stories from many different cultures?

20. Learn about
your school community

OPEN THE DOORS

One child care center I know does an extraordinarily good job of helping children transition into a new class. As part of the process they have the children visit the classroom they will be joining next year.

HELP!

 This is such a good idea, why wait? Help children learn about the community that they are a part of by opening the doors and taking a tour of your building. Do not try to see everything at once. On different days you can choose to visit the office, the basement, the library, or some other interesting area. If you are in a school large enough to have a cafeteria, visit the kitchen and check out the industrial-sized stove, refrigerator, and mixing bowls. If possible, try to arrange some playtime in a nearby (developmentally appropriate) classroom. This can be done when the other class is on the playground, or you and the other teacher could coordinate your schedules and just agree to switch rooms for a time period.

ASK YOURSELF:

Do you help children learn about their community by starting with a tour of their school building?

21. Design events and activities that involve other classes

LET'S TALK TURKEY

Celebrating Thanksgiving at school can be a lot of fun, but it can also be overwhelming. Many schools have large feasts where all the classes get together in one area, and they often invite parents as well. I think young children prefer simpler, more intimate gatherings. Thanksgiving week I would invite the class next door to ours to join us for a snack. We would make cranberry compote. (My Mom had a delicious, simple recipe.) The other class would make sweet potatoes and succotash. It was a very special event. In addition to preparing the food, the children helped move in extra tables and chairs, decorated paper tablecloths, and made centerpieces for the tables.

HELP!

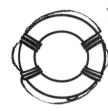 This is a nice way to get to know the people in your building. Invite company all year long, not just at Thanksgiving or other holidays. It's the neighborly thing to do.

I'm sure my Mom would not mind if I share her recipe with you.

Ann's Cranberry Compote

In a large bowl mix:

1 can (16 oz.) whole-berry cranberry sauce

1 can (8 oz.) crushed pineapple (drained)

Chopped walnuts (For the four-year-old class, I would buy large pieces, put them in a plastic bag, and then ask the children to crush the nuts using rolling pins or small hammers. This was a very popular activity; imagine using hammers to prepare food.)

Be careful to check for possible allergic reactions before serving food.

ASK YOURSELF:

Do you help children get to know the other children in the school by doing things together?

Do you invite other classes into your classroom often, not just for special holidays?

22. Invite guests to the classroom

COMPANY'S COMING

During the fall, firefighters are usually available for visits to school programs as part of their Fire Safety Week program.

One year a group of firefighters came to visit. This was an experienced, friendly crew that had done several demonstrations at the local elementary school in the past few weeks. As part of their demonstration they put on their firefighting gear for the children. Wearing their portable air supplies, face masks, helmets, and large boots and carrying axes they looked and sounded rather frightening. They jokingly referred to themselves as "fire monsters." That was all the children needed to hear. Those in my group, who had barely been managing to contain their fears burst into tears at the thought of being in the same room with monsters. All my work telling the children that firefighters were our friends, and that if we had a problem we should go to them, was lost in a single phrase. What obviously had worked so well as a joke in elementary school was frightening to the children in my class.

I had troubling thoughts about the possibility that young children would choose to hide in closets or under beds in burning buildings, rather than go to a Monster Fire Fighter for help.

HELP!

After this incident, even if the guests were very confident about their abilities with young children, I always made sure that we chatted BEFORE they came to visit. Some adults assume four- to eight-year-olds are all the same. They have unreasonable expectations of the young child's ability to sit and listen. I have found guests very appreciative when I go to the trouble to give them a brief synopsis of what we have covered in class and what the children might be interested in hearing and seeing. Most guests love the subject they are going to talk about and need a gentle reminder that very young children have a limited attention span. This advice serves equally well for any field trips you may be planning that involve tour guides.

Before discussing community helpers, talk about the support staff at your school. Invite people who work in your building in to your classroom, and ask them to bring something to show the children. A receptionist could bring colorful index cards, paper clips, or pens. A cook could bring some of the equipment he uses. A delivery person could show her cart, and a maintenance person always has some interesting tools to share. It is a nice gesture to then invite the guests to join the children for snack or lunch. After you have visits from people who work in your building, you can reach out to invite people from the community.

> Talking about community helpers provides a good opportunity to discuss fire safety, traffic and pedestrian safety, and how to respond to potentially dangerous products, objects, or situations. Be sure you deal with these topics in a non-threatening, developmentally appropriate way.

ASK YOURSELF:

Do you invite guests into the classroom to talk about their work?

Do you prepare both the children and the company for the visit?

23. Use dramatic play to help children learn about people in your community

THE THREE LITTLE PIGS

Mrs. Sure was a new teacher at our school. The room she was going to teach in was small and already rather cramped with tables and storage cabinets. However, she insisted that she add one more thing to the room. I was skeptical because of floor space concerns, but decided to give her the benefit of the doubt and see what developed. She added a sturdy wooden structure that resembled a little red schoolhouse. The interior had an area of about four feet by six feet, and the walls were four feet high. It had two cutouts for windows and a front door. It looked like the perfect place to dramatize the story of the three little pigs. During the course of the year that little structure was the focal point of classroom activity. Every three weeks or so, it would be transformed. With a few props, signs, and clever use of shoeboxes that became everything from mailboxes to control panels, the structure was used for many different purposes:

* Barbershop
* Shoe store
* Post office
* Supermarket
* Restaurant
* Pet store
* Office
* Travel agency
* Rocket ship
* Bus
* Television studio

* Movie set
* Photo developing laboratory
* Football locker room
* Recording studio
* Hospital
* Home
* Cave
* Tent in the woods
* And of course the home of the three little pigs

HELP!

Dramatic play is an excellent way for children to experiment with ideas about the different roles people play in the community. By providing a few props you set the stage for children to pretend to be hairstylists, waiters, shopkeepers, bus drivers, police officers, firefighters, dentists, or doctors. Dramatic play gives us a great opportunity to help children overcome sex role stereotypes. Through your positive attitude you let children know that they can do any job that interests them.

Dramatic play is also a good way for children to develop and perfect their social skills. They get experience in leading others and making compromises as they try to understand issues in their life and the lives of those around them.

ASK YOURSELF:

Do you use dramatic play to help children learn about people in their community?

Do you help stimulate dramatic play by varying the materials so they are of interest to all the children, not just to those who enjoy playing in the housekeeping corner?

Do you maintain a gender-neutral attitude when children are engaged in dramatic play?

24. Prepare for field trips

THIRTY TICKETS TO NOWHERE

I thought the very first field trip I was responsible for would be a snap. The teacher of the three-year-olds, an old pro, had planned a train ride for her class. This was something she had done many times in the past, and she invited my class to join her. All I had to do was gather up permission slips and collect the money for the train tickets. The plan was to have parents carpool the children from our school in Maryland to Union Station in Washington, D.C. After dropping us off, the parents would drive their empty cars to the Silver Spring station in Maryland and meet us at an ice-cream parlor next door. After a delicious snack, we would be driven back to school.

As planned, we arrived at Union Station at 9:45 a.m., in plenty of time for the 10:30 train. The parents dropped us off and headed back to Maryland. Since we were so early, we took advantage of the time and toured the station. At 10:10 we went over to the ticket window to purchase our tickets.

 Every child had the exact amount needed for the ticket. I lifted Marcus up to the window, and he asked for a ticket on the 10:30 train to Silver Spring. The ticket agent said, "The next train is at three o'clock." I couldn't believe the response, and told Marcus to ask again. The ticket agent repeated himself: "The next train is at three o'clock."

Realizing something was very wrong, I decided to put Marcus down and deal with this myself. "I want a ticket for the 10:30 a.m. train to Silver Spring." The agent patiently said, "That train was cancelled two months ago; the next train to Silver Spring is at three o'clock this afternoon." I was glad I had put Marcus down as I'm sure I would have dropped him when I finally understood the situation.

Since the parents did not have cell phones (this was in the quiet era before cell phones had been invented), we called the ice-cream parlor where we were supposed to meet the parents for our drive back to school, and explained our situation. We asked the store manager to look for parents who were looking for children, and tell them to drive back to Union Station to pick us up. We wandered about the station looking for interesting activities for the children to observe, and after a while went to the exit to look for our rides home. Eventually the parents arrived and drove us back to school.

HELP!

Some trips require scheduling several months in advance. Even if you have gone on a particular trip many times in past years, it is always wise to reconfirm dates, times, admission fees, parking arrangements, location of bathrooms, and any other necessary details, a week or two before the trip. It is a polite gesture on your part, and may save you from having a memorable experience like my non-train ride.

Field trips are great. The chance to go behind the scenes to see authentic equipment can be very interesting. Think about arranging visits to a dentist's or doctor's office, restaurant, hair salon, bakery, post office, construction site, garden, animal hospital, pet store, animal grooming salon, farm, apiary, photo lab, bicycle repair shop, shoe repair shop, or local theatre. Parents can be very helpful in suggesting people and places to visit.

> A cell phone is something you want to have whenever you are off school grounds. It is also a good idea to arrange for a contact person from school who will be at a specific phone number and can coordinate changes in plans or report delays. This will prove invaluable if problems arise.

ASK YOURSELF:

Do you arrange field trips as part of your curriculum?

Do you PERSONALLY reconfirm arrangements shortly before the trip?

Do you have adequate adult coverage to ensure the children's safety when you take a field trip?

25. Support the inclusion of children who have special needs

MYSTERY PERSON

Six-year-old Fred attended a special education program in the morning and then joined my four-year-old class in the afternoon. During the course of that year I was lucky and had four excellent student teachers work with me, each for a period of eight weeks. After each student teacher had been in the class for a week I told her there was a child who had special needs in the class. I challenged each of the student teachers to observe the children carefully and try to identify the child.

The first child every student teacher chose was a boy who was filled with energy and had some aggression problems. They then guessed it was Gloria, a shy, quiet girl. Often the third choice was another energetic boy in the class, one who was not fluent in English. The guessing would go on for several weeks. Asking the student teachers to try to identify the child who had special needs was a very enlightening experience, not just because of who they chose, but the reasons they gave for their choice. Not one student teacher ever correctly identified Fred as the child who had special needs.

HELP!

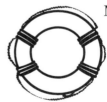 Many teachers incorrectly think of children who have special needs as having major physical deficits or high-energy, negative, aggressive behavior. Clearly there are many children who have special needs who can easily blend into a classroom situation and have a positive influence on all.

ASK YOURSELF:

 Do you believe in inclusion and welcome children who have special needs to your class?

26. Arrange for children who have special needs to participate as much as possible in all activities

BRAVEHEART

Before Debbie joined my four-year-old class I had a conference with her parents. They told me that their daughter had a rare disease that made her muscles weak. The most visible manifestation of this was that she had a tendency to fall down a lot. The parents explained their desire to raise Debbie in as normal a way as possible. They did not treat her differently than they would have if she did not have this disease. They did not stop Debbie from participating in any activities nor did they do anything to make life easier, such as carrying her around in an attempt to move faster or to avoid falls. The father made it very clear that he wanted Debbie to be regarded as any other child in my class. If I made any special arrangements or treated her differently from her classmates, he would immediately withdraw his daughter from school.

Red-headed Debbie was the "go-gettingest" little girl I have ever met. She was filled with spirit and energy. Sometimes walking across the room she would seem to just melt into a puddle on the floor. She would say "Oh drat," crawl to the nearest piece of furniture to pull herself upright, then continue on her way. When I happened to be close by she would use my leg instead of a piece of furniture. She participated in all activities, even attempting to run around with her friends on the playground. When I think about Debbie, the dearest, clearest memory I have is of her going home. Her Dad would pick her up, twirl her around, and then put her on his motorcycle. They would drive off with her long red hair blowing in the breeze.

HELP!

The basic idea of inclusion is to give children who have special needs as normal a school experience as possible. To do this we must be very careful not to draw attention to their problems, but to treat them in as normal a fashion as possible. The teacher is the role model and sets the tone for all in the class. When the children noticed how I let Debbie use my leg to help her get up from the floor they followed my lead. They did not try to lift her or carry her, but if a child was near where she had fallen he stood still so that she could use his body to help her stand up.

There can be a tendency for young children to either reject a child who has special needs, or treat her too lovingly, almost like a baby. It is a delicate balance we must strike between acknowledging the challenges a child who has special needs has to face, and helping her have as normal an experience as possible. We should be compassionate and understanding, but we do not want the deficit to define the child.

They are able who think they are able.

—Virgil

ASK YOURSELF:

Do you help the children who have special needs participate in all class activities to the best of their ability?

Do you role-model an attitude of acceptance?

Do you acknowledge a child's deficits without allowing them to define the child?

Try This

Have the children prepare a special surprise treat for the Director, someone in the office, a maintenance person, or the class next door.

Have children bring in and share photos of family members.

Invite babies, grandparents, and other family members to class.

Have pets visit the classroom.

Invite parents to share recipes or prepare favorite family dishes.

Invite parents to come talk about the work they do.

Create a matching game with pictures of community helpers and the things they use or do at work:
- ☆ Firefighter: fire engine, hose, helmet
- ☆ Hairstylist: comb, scissors, hair dryer
- ☆ Server: menu, tray, dishes of food, notepad
- ☆ Supermarket cashier: cash register, bags, food, household items, wagon

Provide dolls, puppets, and people figures that are representative of different cultures and people who have special needs.

Teach the children simple dances from different cultures.

To help instill a sense of community responsibility and care for the environment:
- ☆ Encourage recycling
- ☆ Ask the children to help clean up the playground

To, Too, Two, Tutu

Providing an Environment and Experiences That Promote Literacy

Children must learn to read because we read to learn. Teaching children to read is a formidable task, and does get a great deal of attention in most schools. However, there is a vital component that is sometimes overlooked. With some children the real challenge is not teaching them how to read but teaching them to WANT to read.

The pleasure that comes from reading a good book, the sense of satisfaction that we get when we learn something new, or the joy of discovering information about faraway places needs to be communicated to children, and should be developed and reinforced every bit as much as promoting phonological awareness. If reading is a pleasure, like listening to music or watching a sporting event, then children will do it on their own. If it is just another skill they have learned in school, then they will read reluctantly and only what a teacher assigns, and no more. A tremendous source of pleasure, entertainment, and knowledge will be closed off to them. Having the skill without the enthusiasm is like having a birthday cake without the icing.

> *There is more treasure in books than in all the pirate's loot on Treasure Island . . . and best of all, you can enjoy these riches every day of your life.*
>
> *—Walt Disney*

27. Read to children frequently, regardless of their age

IT'S NEVER TOO EARLY

As a volunteer with the Read Aloud program, I would spend one morning each week reading books to individual children in the three-year-old class of a child care center. It always made me feel good that when I arrived three or four children would immediately line up near the book corner and literally push and shove for their turn to select books that I would then read to them. Sadly there were also a few children who avoided me, and the books that I brought, like the plague. They would scurry to the other side of the room and get busy with trucks or other toys. Occasionally, I could coax some of the reluctant children to sit and look at a book for just a few moments, but without the benefit of a seatbelt, they never stayed for more than one book. While it is possible that the children were trying to avoid contact with me, I believe it is more likely that they were trying to avoid the activity I represented. It is troubling that at the tender age of three they had already decided that they didn't like books and wanted nothing to do with them.

HELP!

In every group of children there are a few who literally rush to hear a story read, and others who run equally as fast in the opposite direction to avoid it.

Children who are read to frequently from an early age understand the pleasures inherent in reading a book. My mother read to me often. However, my Dad left school after the fifth grade and as a result was insecure about his ability to "correctly" read books. He did it very rarely; yet it is his reading that I recall most vividly. I did not care about his reading style, only the warmth and secure feeling I felt as I curled up next to him.

The undivided attention of an adult reading a book to a young child is emotionally rewarding. It is a bonding experience, cozy, warm, and calming. The voice of an adult reading a book to a child is different from the one used when engaged in a normal conversation. It is soothing and expressive, almost like singing. We need to recognize the importance of reading to young children, because it helps them form positive attitudes about books and reading in the future. I do not believe any age is too early to hold a child close and read to him, but I can say that at three years old it is almost too late.

> You may have tangible wealth untold;
> Caskets of jewels and coffers of gold.
> Richer than I you can never be—
> I had a mother who read to me.
>
> —Strickland Gillilan

ASK YOURSELF:

Do you read to children frequently, even when they are too young to understand what you are reading?

Do you encourage parents to read to their children every day?

28. Enrich your book corner

BEYOND STORYBOOKS

When I went to the library to freshen up the supply of books for my book corner I would usually pick the classic stories such as *Peter's Chair*, *Goodnight Moon*, or *Anansi the Spider*. On one particular visit I was having very bad luck. It was as though locusts had descended and picked the shelves bare. In desperation I wandered around in a different section of the library. I came upon some books that had great pictures. The books had text that appeared to be geared to eight- or nine-year-olds, but what wonderful photographs. I gathered up a wide assortment, books on everything from insects and seashells to reptiles and volcanoes.

HELP!

The children loved these books! They studied the pictures with great enthusiasm. The pictures in the books formed the basis for some interesting discussions. If I was asked to read the book, I found that the captions beneath the pictures served very well. From that point on, I did not limit my book corner collection only to preschool storybooks.

♦ You should have a well-stocked book corner with a generous supply of developmentally appropriate books that are rotated frequently. Supplementing your library with a few advanced books that have interesting pictures is a good idea, but these cannot take the place of preschool storybooks.

♦ Select developmentally appropriate preschool story books that:

Enrich children's language and promote phonological awareness

Support diversity and inclusion through text and illustrations

Are predictable and easy for children to understand

Allow children to join in through sound effects or by repeating refrains

Before teaching about pets, insects, firefighters, or anything else, I would prepare myself by reading a book on the topic that was aimed at an eight-year-old reader (usually 20 easy pages). Using this little trick, I could answer most of the questions a preschool child would ask me on any given subject from Ants to Zinnias.

ASK YOURSELF:

Do you provide an ample supply of stimulating books on different levels and topics for the children to look at?

Do you rotate the books regularly?

Do you prepare yourself by reading about subjects that you are going to teach?

29. Provide activities that help children develop visual discrimination

THE GARDEN

The last place in the world I thought about developing visual discrimination skills was on the playground. After we planted our garden and watered it very carefully every day, I found we were growing more weeds than carrots or radishes. I decided to invite the children to do the weeding. Of course they were very concerned, as I was, that they not mistake a carrot or radish plant for an unwanted weed. The children were very intense as they studied the size and shape of the various leaves in the garden, trying to determine which ones should be left and which should be pulled.

HELP!

This is a great visual discrimination exercise. A number of children who would never sit and do puzzles were more than willing to spend the morning sorting out leaf patterns in the garden. Once again I rediscovered the lesson that for young children learning takes place wherever they get involved.

You cannot learn to read without developing the skill of visual discrimination. After all, to the untrained eye the differences between c and e, d and b or E and F can be very subtle. Activities such as weeding, puzzles, and matching games help children learn to notice subtle differences.

To the uneducated, an A is just three sticks.

—A. A. Milne

ASK YOURSELF:

Do you provide puzzles and matching games for the children to use?

Do you provide other activities that encourage visual discrimination?

30. Provide an environment that is rich with letters

DON'T BURY THAT RECIPE IN A CLOSET

When I had a cooking activity scheduled, I usually pulled out the recipe chart, put it on an easel, and with the children read the directions for whatever we were going to make or cook. My normal routine was to put the chart away at the end of the activity. WHAT A WASTE! I would spend hours carefully printing and trying to illustrate a recipe, and it saw the light of day for about three hours.

One day when I was particularly slow at getting around to putting the recipe chart away the children gathered in front of it and reminisced about what they had done. One child looked for the illustration of raisins and proudly said, "I did that." Another said, pointing to the appropriate location, "Look. I added the cup of water." They were reading the chart on their own.

HELP!

Don't forget the purpose of a recipe chart. You do not spend hours carefully printing directions so the adult doesn't forget how to make muffins or play dough. You are creating a reading experience for the children. Leave the chart up at the children's eye level. Many will take a second look at it. I have even had some children use it as a reference when they wanted to know how to write a particular letter.

♦ Charts are teaching tools that help children recognize letters and encourage the process of learning to read. When making a chart, use only one color for the printed word. This will help children see the letters clearly and become familiar with text—the words and the spaces between words. Of course pictures and decorations should be added around the edges to make it attractive, but if it is a teaching tool the letters should be plain and clear. Remember K.I.S.S.—Keep it simple, sweetheart.

♦ Make signs and place them at appropriate locations in the classroom; for example, Chair, Door, Stove (housekeeping corner), Books, Blocks. Use signs on the playground, such as Slide, One Way, No Parking, and Stop.

ASK YOURSELF:

Do you display recipe charts and leave them up for the children to look at after the project has been completed?

Do you make charts that are printed in a clear and simple manner in order to make letter recognition easy for children?

Do you provide an environment rich with letters?

31. Display charts and pictures at the children's eye level

WHERE YOU STAND AFFECTS WHAT YOU SEE

Many years ago I visited one of the world's great art museums. It was literally bursting at the seams with wonderful paintings. In an attempt to display as much artwork as possible, they crowded all the available wall space with paintings. There were several rooms where the masterpieces were displayed in three or more rows, starting at eye level and going clear up to the ceiling. I found this frustrating. Only a giant could have seen the top two rows. I think they should have provided ladders or at least binoculars—those ceilings were pretty high.

HELP!

Time after time I go into classrooms where the helper chart, calendar, and other important reading material is so high (from a child's perspective) that it might as well be on the ceiling—or not displayed at all. A simple test of sitting down on the floor, as a child would, and then looking around the room will give you a whole new perspective. What can you see from down there? What catches your eye? What letters or pictures are just too small to really notice? Are some things too small to see from a distance?

If the charts and calendar are made for the adults, they can be hung high on the wall. If they are made for the children, so they can read their name or the job they are doing this week, then it is only fair to lower it to THEIR eye level. After all, they are not giraffes.

ASK YOURSELF:

Do you display charts and pictures at the children's eye level?

32. Print letters in a consistent manner

MY NAME

In most school settings nametags are used the first week of school, until the staff learns all the names. I worked in a center where to facilitate observation by students and researchers the children wore nametags all year long. After a few weeks all the children could readily find their nametag in the bin. By the start of winter, children would grab a handful of nametags and delight in reading them and distributing them to their rightful owners. This reading of nametags stimulated a lot of interest in letters and reading.

HELP!

Initially, I would draw a little symbol on the nametag, such as a ball or hat, and I would write the name in green, blue, or red, which would act as an additional clue to help the child who was not familiar with the letters of the alphabet. However, when it was time to repair/replace the nametag (several weeks later), I could usually remove this support and write the name in basic black.

When asked by a child to write her name on a piece of artwork, adults should consider it a great teaching opportunity. Turn the paper over so you can use as much space as needed (as opposed to the small crunched name usually written in a corner of the paper) and boldly print the child's name using upper and lower case letters. Print as though the child and not adults were meant to read the name. It is a good idea to say the letters as you carefully print them.

♦ When the child wants to write her name by herself, you can help by writing her name on a separate piece of paper so she can refer to it. You also can stimulate interest in writing by providing examples of other words that children might want to write, such as Mommy or Daddy.

♦ Since books are printed using both upper and lower case letters, it is important for children to become familiar with all the letters used. Teachers should post a correctly printed alphabet in the room for use by both the children and the staff. While commercially produced alphabet charts are attractive, they often do not represent what the children will be expected to learn in the local school district. Copies of the alphabet should also be sent home to the parents to ensure that all the adults are consistent in the way they print letters. This is no place for individual creativity, since different versions of how to print letters will only confuse the children.

ASK YOURSELF:

Do you provide opportunities for the children to see their names in print?

Do you help children learn to write by providing examples that they can copy?

Do you and the other adults print letters in a consistent manner to avoid confusing the children?

33. Create opportunities for children to read and write their names

SIGN ON THE DOTTED LINE

In February, when time indoors seemed to be endlessly expanded because of cold weather conditions, I would try to bring special activities into the classroom. By far the most popular was the workbench. Every morning there was a mad dash by the children to get there first. Almost everyone wanted a turn, and it was hard keeping track of who was next. Children became irritable, not quite sure if it was their turn yet. Standing too close to the workbench, pushing, and shoving were all becoming problems. It was getting so complex that in desperation I walked around with a list in my pocket, so when asked I could check to see who had the next turn. Even this didn't seem to satisfy the children.

HELP!

I then created a sign up sheet, put it on a clipboard, and posted it near the workbench. Even those who could not recognizably write their name could at least make a "mark" that they remembered, and just as important the other children recognized. It was a great solution. Now the responsibility of who had the next turn was the children's. When curious as to how long it might be before they could use the bench, they would check the sheet and count the names ahead of their own. Some children even took it upon themselves to notify the next child on the list when it was his turn.

Talk about positive reinforcement to learn to write your name, or read other names. This was so satisfying to the children that they suggested we do the same thing for turns on tricycles and other highly prized activities. They could trust the written word not to change, and could check on it themselves during the course of the day. This gave them confidence and a feeling of being in control. (What a sense of power!) Reading the sign-up sheet to see who was doing what and when became an important activity. The staff had a great pressure taken off their shoulders. The children had assumed the responsibility of who had the next turn and were experiencing firsthand the benefits of reading and writing.

Remember that too much of a good thing can turn sour. The sign-up sheet should not become a way of life; it is a good tool to be used on occasion. If overused, free play can become too structured.

ASK YOURSELF:

Do you provide meaningful opportunities for the children to read and write their names?

34. Encourage reading and writing everywhere

DANGER!!!

I'm sure you have known a few children like Juan and Thomas. They would spend every spare moment in the block corner. Getting them to the art table was almost impossible—unless we were making airplanes or trucks.

One morning as I sat on the floor watching them build a particularly complex structure I asked them if they wanted to tell me about it. With great enthusiasm and drama, Thomas said, "This is a secret place, and in this building there are bombs and dynamite." I replied that that sounded pretty dangerous to me. He nodded his head in agreement. I asked if he would like a sign on the building that said "Danger" so people would know to be extra careful. This idea really pleased both boys and I went off to gather up scissors, paper, markers,  and tape, and then brought my goodies back to the block area. The small (three-inch) sign that I made looked very official as we taped it to the side of a block. Then the boys decided they needed another sign for the other building, and a stop sign for the road. Before you knew it, sign making became the major project of the morning.

The next day they built an airport and asked me to come over and create the appropriate signs. Runway, Tower, One Way, Tickets and, of course, the ever-popular Danger were requested. This pattern of building and writing signs went on for the rest of the year. On days when I was too busy to get over to the blocks, the children decided to create their own signs. By the end of the year almost every child in the class could read and write the words Danger, Stop, Do Not Enter, and One Way.

HELP!

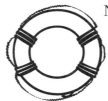 Not all writing needs to happen at a table. The children treasured their signs and would often tape them to their shirts and wear them all day. The little added attraction of taping signs onto a block project became a major teaching tool for the rest of the year.

> If children won't come to paper and pencil activities, let's bring the paper and pencil activities to them.

ASK YOURSELF:

Do you provide reading and writing opportunities throughout the classroom or only at the art table?

35. When children show an interest in letters, help them take the next step

T IS FOR TIARA

Ms. Opportunity started circle time by showing flash cards with the children's names printed on them. When a child recognized his name, he was supposed to say, "Here." It was her way of taking attendance. The order was the same each day, and the children were not very interested. The name Trevor was displayed and Tiara became all excited—she was one of the few children paying attention. She said, "That's me, I'm here." The teacher replied, "This says Trevor." "Uh-uh," said Tiara, "That's me." The teacher again said, "No, this is Trevor and he is not here today." Now agitated, Tiara got off her seat, went up to the card, pointed to the T and said, "That's Tiara." The teacher again said, "No, it's Trevor, and you need to sit down."

HELP!

At this point I was cringing and thinking to myself, "Why doesn't the teacher point out the other letters to Tiara, the ones that come after the T?" It was the perfect moment to help Tiara take the next step. She was focused on *T*, but ready to go beyond that. I love it when a child like Steve notices the sign on the toy stove that says "stove" and declares that that is his name! I compliment him on his keen eyesight, and then point out the other letters that make all the difference. The same learning opportunities can happen for Mike when he notices the M on the milk carton, or when Wilma notices that the Wednesday on the calendar starts just like her name.

> Children let you know when they are ready to take the next step. If your environment is stimulating and has letters and materials at their eye level, the possibilities are endless.

ASK YOURSELF:

Do you take advantage and build on the opportunity presented when a child shows an interest in letters?

Do you help children reach for the next level?

36. Create activities that involve letter recognition

DO I HAVE A "B"?

Getting out to the playground in an orderly fashion in the wintertime is a major challenge. The skill level at which children put on ski pants, boots, sweaters, mittens, and hats varies considerably. Of course the quickest one to dress is always the child who can get into the most mischief. To address the problem of wandering mischief makers I asked the children who were dressed in their winter gear to sit and wait at the table until the other children were ready.

When all the children were ready, or enough that one adult could go outside while the other stayed in to complete the dressing, I needed to think of ways to get the children to move in an orderly fashion from the table to the playground. A group of children dressed in heavy snow gear racing to the door is not a pretty sight. I used many of the standard line-up techniques: "If you are wearing the color red, if you have brown eyes, if you have short hair, if . . . , you may go to the door."

HELP!

One variation that I used was to call out letters: "If your name starts with a B, if your name starts with an S." Taken a step farther, "If your name has an A or a D in it." You could literally see the children visualizing their names as they tried to figure out if they had the correct letter. On several occasions children would poke their friends and tell them that they had the letter in question, and should go to the door. If a child wasn't sure, I would write her name out on a piece of paper, and we would look for the right letter. This activity sparked a high interest in letters. The children had a very real reason to want to know how to spell their names. Some were so enthusiastic that they learned the letters of their last name as well. After all, that did increase their odds of getting to the door faster.

ASK YOURSELF:

Do you develop games and provide opportunities for children to use their knowledge of letters in a positive, meaningful way?

37. Help children develop phonological awareness by making the connection between printed letters and sounds

READ ANYTHING FIT TO PRINT

Every now and then a three-year-old child would sit down and write some letters on a paper. When I noticed this I would make a point of reading aloud what he had written. This is more challenging than you realize. How would you pronounce "abcdlimbytoxyzzzzz" or "rrammmnaal"? The children would laugh themselves silly as I struggled to read what they had written. They couldn't wait to write longer and longer words to see me get all tongue-tied, and I couldn't find a better way to encourage them to keep right on printing letters.

HELP!

Some of the best learning opportunities are child, not adult, initiated. Provide a rich environment that includes paper, crayons, and pencils and then be ready to reinforce the activities the children are drawn to. In addition to encouraging writing, this activity also gives you the opportunity to increase phonological awareness. When reading the letters slide your finger along under the letters as you pronounce them. This will help the children see that each letter represents a sound. Be sure this remains a silly, fun game. The moment you let it become a serious lesson the children will lose interest and want to walk away.

ASK YOURSELF:

Do you have paper, crayons, and pencils readily available for children over two years old to use?

Do you encourage and pick up on the children's activities and interests?

Do the children in your class perceive writing as a fun activity, or is it an adult-imposed chore?

38. Play games that involve phonics

READ WITH YOUR EARS

When a child would look at the calendar and declare, "Sam and Saturday are the same," meaning they both started with S, I would get enthusiastic and quickly reinforce this observation with a long list of S words. "Yes, you are right, and so are Sarah, Steve, Sally, Sophie, sauce, soap, soup, soda, sew, star, and stick." I would continue as long as I could (J was tough and, of course, X is just about impossible). When children were ready they would happily join in the silly game I was playing. Sometimes they clearly understood the logic but could not think of a word and would then invent one like "siler," "suder," or whatever began with the appropriate letter we were using. It was a beautiful moment as I observed them make the connection between letters and sounds.

HELP!

I believe we learn to read with our ears as well as our eyes. A good understanding of phonics is very important when learning to read. Be ready to take advantage of the moment. When children start showing an interest in letters, we should provide the environment that fosters and expands their interest.

♦ Another game you can play with children is rhyming. Start off by saying, "hat, rat, and fat," and then invite the child to say a word. If they say "sugar," smile and say that's a nice word too. Do not tell them that it is wrong, or try to explain that they don't understand. This puts pressure on them, which you definitely do not want to do. Eventually they will hear the rhyme and catch on, and then go on to even create new words of their own to rhyme with yours.

Poetry is an excellent way to expose children to phonetic similarities and differences. It has a playful approach to language that children enjoy. Classics such as Mother Goose Nursery Rhymes, books by Dr. Seuss, and popular finger plays such as "Ten Little Monkeys Jumping on the Bed" should be recited to the children frequently, and by all means encourage the children to join in.

ASK YOURSELF:

Do you play rhyming and word games with children to help them develop phonological awareness?

Do you read poetry to the children regularly?

39. Develop comprehension skills by asking thoughtful questions

PHONICS ALONE IS NOT ENOUGH

Would you please read the following out loud:

> Quando a câmera está para ser utilizada no modo de focagem automática, a lente foca automaticamente. Durante a operação de auto focagem, o anel de focagem rodará e o seu movimento não deverá ser impedido.

Excellent! You read that very well. By now you should be saying, "Yes, but what does it mean? What did I read?"

HELP!

The problem with teaching just phonics is that there is no comprehension. The above example of reading in a foreign language makes that easier to understand. After all, you did read it.

I can still recall reading a high school textbook late at night. I knew I had read the page, but I couldn't tell you a thing about what I had just read. In order to comprehend, we have to be involved and alert. We have to THINK as we read. Question, anticipate, and try to understand where the author is leading us. Without our mind actively involved, we might as well be reading Portuguese. (That is the language you just read.) It is important to teach children the skill of being actively involved with the text.

Asking questions during the telling/reading of a story will help accomplish this. Not questions of fact like, "What color is the coat?" but questions of conjecture: "How would you solve the problem? What do you think will happen next? Is that a good idea? Why?" Let's help children learn to think as they are entertained. If we can get them into the habit of being alert and engaged in the story, then maybe they won't fall asleep reading that high school textbook as I did.

Have some logical guesses about what you read in Portuguese? The translation is as follows: "When the camera is in the auto focus mode, the lens focuses automatically. During auto focus operation, the focusing ring will rotate and its movement should not be hindered." Some of the instructions for this camera were incomprehensible to me even in English!

ASK YOURSELF:

Do you ask thought-provoking questions when reading a book?

40. Create original books for the children to read

FIRST READER

Children like nothing better than looking at pictures of themselves and their friends, which is no different from the adults I know. During the course of the year I took a lot of photographs. To protect and preserve the pictures I put them in an album. This became the most popular book in the class. Children spent a great deal of time poring over the photos, giggling, talking, and reminiscing.

HELP!

Clearly, anything that is this popular and gets so much attention can be made into a powerful teaching tool. I decided to add captions under each photograph in the class album. Very simple sentences such as:

Ben and Nicole like to play.

Eva, Javier, and Patrick like to run.

Anthony, Emma, and Shanel like to read.

Look at Beverly play.

I tried to keep the vocabulary very limited. The most frequently used words were *run, play,* and *like.* The children loved to see their own names and quickly started picking out the names of friends, and then moved on to recognizing words such as play. The children were learning some base words other than Exit and Stop. I had in fact created their first reader. Every few months I would add more photos and captions.

> If you create a class album, be sure that every child is clearly visible in several of the photos.

My older son's favorite book was a collection of postcards and photographs that I had assembled in a photo album. Under each picture, I wrote a simple sentence, such as, "This is a train." It was an easy task to create a book with things I knew he liked.

ASK YOURSELF:

 Do you create simple books for the children to read?

41. Encourage children to create their own books

MAKE A BOOK

Another February activity that went well was book making. I would take a few sheets of paper (about four by six inches) and staple them together. I would then ask the children if they would like to make a book. They would draw things on several pages and then come to the adult to dictate a story. To get things started I would offer up, "Once upon a time" (not too original, but the children felt right at home with it).

HELP!

 The results of this activity were fascinating. Some of the children were much more interested in watching the adult write down the words that they were saying than in drawing the pictures. As a matter of fact, they would scribble a few colors on each page in a hurry to get to the good part— dictating the story. Usually the plot lines were the familiar fairy tales, but every now and then we did get an original creation. The most interesting development was that the children began to read their books to one another. Some children would ask an adult to read books written by several of their classmates. They liked this activity so much that they would continue to request it long after the snows had melted.

> Children are most interested in what they create. Reading your very own story is a thrill (even for adults).

ASK YOURSELF:

Do you provide the materials and the kind of supportive environment that encourages children to create their own stories and books?

Do you make yourself available to write things the children wish to dictate?

Try This

Decorate index cards to create simple matching games. Draw two of each item. Children can match colors, shapes, designs, objects, letters, names, and when ready, words.

When returning completed art work that is ready to go home, hold up each item to see if the children can read the name and identify the artist.

If a child is interested, you can offer to write his comments on a drawing or painting that he has created. For example, This is my brother, This is a storm, or This is Grandma's house. Be careful not to press the child to make comments, as art work is often not representational but just experimental at this age.

Have the class develop a pen pal relationship. This does not have to be with someone in another country or state. You can get something going with a friend in a nearby center.

Include children in correspondence. Invite them to write, contribute ideas or decorate the paper:
   ☆ Let children help prepare invitations and thank you notes
   ☆ Encourage children to make and send birthday cards

Create experience charts where children contribute their ideas.

After you have read a few books to a child in a cozy and relaxed atmosphere, ask the child to read to you. Tell the child, "You can read the pictures." The child can then take charge, hold the book, turn the pages, and read the pictures to you. Start this activity with books the child has seen before. It can be even more challenging if after a few successes you introduce a book that the child is not familiar with. The children's stories can be wonderfully creative or inane, but reading gives them a sense of power, even if they are only reading the pictures.

Modify the popular children's game Candyland to make it increasingly more challenging. Replace a few of the cards with ones you make. Write a color word on a card using the matching color. For example, write the word red with a red Magic Marker or blue with a blue Magic Marker. When the children are ready for more of a challenge you can write some of the color words using only a black Magic Marker. Be careful not to make the game too difficult; children should still enjoy playing it.

Once Upon a Time

Story/Group Time With Young Children

Advancements in technology have brought wonderful conveniences and labor-saving devices into our everyday world. One improvement that causes me great concern is the TV remote control. I admit being able to hit the mute button or change channels during an obnoxious commercial is a positive. On the other hand, I fondly remember the good old days, when a commercial break wasn't seen as a time to surf channels, but rather as an opportunity to talk to others in the room or race to the refrigerator, cookie jar, or bathroom, depending on the most immediate need at the moment.

At home I often flip back and forth between television shows or movies and wind up seeing bits and pieces of each, but nothing in its entirety. When I'm at a movie theater, if the movie seems a bit dull or slow, I find myself instinctively reaching for the remote control in a futile attempt to fast forward through the dull part or change channels. I am concerned that the ability to flip stations is having a negative effect on my attention span. I find I have become less patient, and I fear I am not alone. This can't be good.

As educators concerned with the future of society, we recognize how damaging a short attention span can be to children. It takes concentration, time, and effort to understand and appreciate difficult concepts. The ability to listen and focus for more than a 20-second sound-bite is crucial to individual success in school and work. We must help children break free of the TV remote control attention span syndrome. Story/group time encourages children to focus and increase their attention span. For this reason it is more important than ever before.

42. Keep group time interesting

RESERVED SEATING

It seemed as though every time I went into Mrs. Rut's classroom she was trying a new seating arrangement for group time. In the beginning of the year the children would just cluster in a group on the carpet. The first rearrangement was chairs placed in a semi-circle. Within two days of this new set up, the children were busy falling off, rocking, or squirming on their chairs. It is amazing how creative and mobile some children can be in their interaction with a chair.

Her next attempt to control the inattentive children was to give them small pieces of cloth that they were supposed to sit on. These quickly became major distractions that were curled, rolled, hidden, wrapped around arms and heads, and even tossed about the room. To overcome the problems of using pieces of cloth, Mrs. Rut cleverly decided to just use tape on the floor. Each child had an "X" to sit on. You guessed it, within a day or two the children were busy peeling the tape up off the floor instead of paying attention at group time.

HELP!

Some teachers focus on seating arrangements. They carefully adjust things so that the inattentive, high-energy child is sandwiched in between two quiet, calm children. They hope that somehow this will keep him in check, but it doesn't really work. There is no magic seating plan for group time, and there is no need for one. If the lessons are developmentally appropriate, interesting, stimulating, and most important, varied, then regardless of the seating arrangement, children will stay focused and attentive.

While regular routines are important, group time problems will occur if you keep doing exactly the same thing day after day. It is so boringly predictable. You probably have a favorite dinner, but if you had to eat only that for 10 days in a row, you would lose your appetite. (Maybe I should write a diet book.) The answer is not to change the seating arrangement but to change your lesson plans and shake things up now and then.

The keys to successful, productive group times are:

Vary the material you present

Have the children actively participate as much as possible

Be careful that your group times are not too long for the attention span of the children

ASK YOURSELF:

Do you focus on seating arrangements rather than how and what you are presenting to the children?

Do you vary what you present?

Do you ask the children questions and encourage them to participate in group time?

Do you keep your group times short and tailored to the attention span of the children?

43. Use props or songs to attract the children

EVERYBODY ON THE RUG

Ms. Yell wanted to start group time. She issued her usual invitation, which consisted of calling out, "Everybody on the rug now." The children heard her, but many chose to ignore her. She raised her voice and repeated herself in the hopes that a few more children would go over to the rug so she could start group time.

HELP!

When you want the children to gather in a specific location go there, and then use songs, finger plays, pictures, a puppet, toys, a guessing game, or a surprise bag (a pillowcase with an object inside) to draw them to you. These work like a magnet to attract the children. They are naturally curious, and that is the key to getting them to join group time.

Some children may not be developmentally ready to sit in a group situation. Rather than insisting that they join the group, allow them to play quietly nearby. Over time you will discover that they are listening from a distance and will eventually drift toward the group activity.

ASK YOURSELF:

Do you use songs, finger plays, puppets, or other attention-getting devices when trying to get children to gather for group time?

44. Start your story promptly

EYES ON ME

Have you ever noticed at the movie theater that there is a discernible mumble of chatter in the audience during the coming attractions? No one seems to mind much as everyone understands that the main attraction, or important part of the entertainment, has not yet begun. Once the feature film begins, most audiences quickly settle down and focus on the movie.

With great frequency one hears teachers use the phrase, "All eyes on me." Another common, but equally foolish phrase is, "I can't start the story until everyone is looking at me." It's even worse when the teacher says, "John, I won't begin the story until you are looking at me." Now John, instead of the teacher, is in control. He has the power to delay the start of the story by misbehaving and looking elsewhere—a very tempting power trip.

HELP!

Children realize when "the feature film" is beginning. We have to guard against investing too much energy and time in waiting for every single child to be focused on the teacher. Let the story do its magic. When the children are basically calmed down, and only a few stragglers are not quite settled in, I immediately start the story. If the book was well chosen, then the children will be drawn to it. You do not have to demand the children's attention, it will come naturally.

> Adults often forget that children have a limited attention span. If you spend too long introducing your subject, you may be sabotaging your own lesson. Cut to the chase. Remember, children's attention spans are definitely limited so use time wisely.

ASK YOURSELF:

Do you wait for every single child to be settled before starting to read, or do you start promptly and let the story draw them in?

45. Sit where all the children can see you and make individual eye contact

"I CAN'T SEE"

The three-year-old class was gathered on the rug and Ms. Cold began her group time. Harold called out, "I can't see" and Ms. Cold thoughtfully turned in his direction. Victor then called out, "I can't see," and so Ms. Cold now turned more toward Victor. When Nina chimed in, "I can't see," the frustrated teacher replied, "Just open your eyes more."

HELP!

As sure as the sun rises every day, teachers in preschool classrooms will hear the complaint of a child who says, "I can't see." Usually once verbalized, several other children join in the chorus. Isn't it amazing how they develop this problem, regardless of their respective locations, and all at the same time? I believe that this is a child's way of expressing something far more complex than the ability to see.

When a child says "I can't see," he usually means "Can you still see me?" He is feeling the pressure of being in a group situation and craves some sort of recognition. He literally feels lost in the crowd. The simplest solution to this problem is a smile, nod of the head, eye contact, and a slight elevation of the book, picture, or other materials you are using.

> While an adult sitting on the floor with a group of children is cozy, if the group is too large there really can be a legitimate problem seeing. In that case, use a low chair that keeps you close to the children, but still provides enough elevation so that all can easily see. That way when you hear the inevitable "I can't see," you know it is a child feeling the pressure of other children and seeking a little recognition, rather than having a problem seeing.

When a teacher asks the question, "Can everybody see?" she is unwittingly inviting a crush of children (as they move forward) to whatever she is showing, whether it's seashells, rocks, or a flannel board story. Don't ask. If they can't see, they will do something about it. Children naturally inch closer to something they want a better look at.

ASK YOURSELF:

Do you elevate the book or objects you are showing high enough that all the children can easily see?

Do you try to make eye contact, and/or touch individual children to help ease the pressure they may be feeling at group time?

Do you ask the children if they can see, which disrupts your lesson as they try to move closer?

46. Be aware of what is going on behind you

BEHIND YOUR BACK

Ms. Oblivious was having trouble getting the children to focus on the picture she was holding in her hand. The lunch cart had just been rolled into the room behind her, and watching the food being prepared was just too interesting.

HELP!

 You cannot see what is going on behind you, but the children can. When conducting group time, make sure the children won't be distracted by any activity that may be going on behind you. Try to place yourself in front of a wall or in a corner so you will have the children's undivided attention.

ASK YOURSELF:

 Do you carefully select where you position yourself for group time?

Do you try to eliminate any distractions by asking others in the room to minimize their activity level?

47. Put on a show at story time

BE A HAM

Four-year-old Keisha's favorite activity was pretending to be a teacher. She would gather together a handful of dolls or stuffed animals and place them carefully on the carpet. She then selected a book and began "reading" it to her willing audience. Keisha read with great drama and flare, and she considerately paused now and then to show her students the pictures. (It was a surreal experience to see her pretending to be me.) She did such a good job that it was not unusual for a real child to come over, join the stuffed animals, and listen to the story.

HELP!

Keisha had the right idea. We should tell stories with enthusiasm, gesture, drama, and sound effects. For instance, for the story of the "Three Billy Goats Gruff" you could have three different surfaces to tap on with a stick for each of the goats as they walk across the bridge. When reading or telling a story, it is almost like putting on a performance, and in this instance it is fine to be a bit of a ham.

With older children you can also tell stories using minimal or no visual props at all. The less there is to look at, the more children can rely on their own imagination to create the characters or places in your story. Staying with the example of the story of the "Three Billy Goats Gruff," use only an illustration of the billy goats and leave the troll up to the imagination of the children.

Good teaching is one-fourth preparation and three-fourths pure theatre.

—Gail Godwin

ASK YOURSELF:

Do you read stories in an interesting and entertaining fashion, using your hands and face as well as your voice to communicate?

Do you, on occasion, tell stories using just a few pictures or props in order to encourage the children to use their imagination?

48. Tell, don't read, flannel board stories

ALL FALL DOWN

Ms. Effort worked very hard preparing a flannel board story. The children were excited as they saw the board being set up. Ms. Effort then balanced the flannel board figures and a huge curriculum guidebook on her lap. She placed the first figure on the board and immediately got distracted looking for a particular page in the book. When she found the page she began reading, "Once upon a time there was a lonely teacup that met a spoon." She then had to put the book down, trying to hold it open to the correct page, while she fumbled around in her lap trying to locate the flannel board spoon. Needless to say this was rather distracting, and after a few more additions to the plot line, the book and the remaining flannel board figures slipped off her lap completely. Once again, she had to locate the correct page in the book. The children were finding the sideshow of falling items far more entertaining than the flannel board story.

HELP!

The whole purpose of a flannel board story is to free you from the printed word. Without a book we can have better eye contact with the children, the flexibility to emphasize, shorten, or lengthen parts of the story, and have our hands free to make gestures. If the plot is so complicated that we can't remember it, or the verse so poetic that we want to read it, then it is a poor selection to use as a flannel board story. If absolutely necessary, you can jot down some key words on a five-by-eight index card to remind you of a particular phrase or plot twist, but please do not read a flannel board story. Reading books and telling stories should be two distinctly different experiences.

Flannel boards usually come with rather flimsy stands and need to be set up on a table. The floor is just too low. I have experienced my share of flannel boards tumbling over at the most inopportune moments. Putting the flannel board on a paint easel is a good solution to the crashing/sliding flannel board problem. It is the right height and is portable enough to be put anywhere in the room. (Obviously the paint jars should be removed first.) A unit block placed in one of the jar holders on the shelf will keep the board from slipping to the floor.

ASK YOURSELF:

Do you take advantage of the increased opportunities available for gestures and story modification when using flannel board stories?

Do you TELL flannel board stories rather than just read them?

49. Create original flannel board stories

MY MENAGERIE

I always had trouble finding good Thanksgiving stories, and one year I decided to create my own Thanksgiving flannel board story. Due to my distinct lack of artistic skill I looked for the easiest way to do this. As I gave it some thought, I realized I could take the pig from the story of the "Three Little Pigs," grab a goat from the "Three Billy Goats Gruff," and use the cow from the "Ask Mister Bear" story. By re-circulating these old figures, half my work was already done.

HELP!

When creating flannel board figures, try to make them universally interchangeable, regardless of the story. By making them to scale (e.g., the bird is smaller than the cat, the dog is smaller than the cow, and children are somewhere in between the size of a dog and cow) you will increase their utility. When you create all-purpose cows, dogs, and birds, you don't have to produce a new one for each story. To keep things fresh, make new human beings for each story; that is a far easier task than making all new figures every time.

I can attest to the fact that with reasonable care (stored in a manila envelope) these figures can last 20 years or more. Making flannel board figures is a very worthwhile investment of your time.

> Nothing delights children more than an original story about them, their family, pets, or whatever. Charles Dodgson (pen name: Lewis Carroll), a mathematician at Oxford University, created *Alice's Adventures in Wonderland* to entertain Alice Liddell, the daughter of a friend.

Make flannel board figures for the children to use to create stories of their own.

ASK YOURSELF:

Do you create original flannel board stories?

Do you have flannel board figures for the children to use?

50. Choose books that are developmentally appropriate to read to a group

ONE SIZE DOES NOT FIT ALL

Ms. Lazy taught the two-year-old class on Tuesday and Thursday and the four-year-old group on Monday, Wednesday, and Friday. When I visited her two-year-old group on Tuesday she was attempting to read the same book she had read to the four-year-old class the day before. There was a lot of squirming, restlessness, and inattention. She wisely decided to stop reading the book. She cheerfully said, "Okay that's enough for today; we can finish the book on Thursday."

HELP!

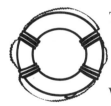

Trying to read a lengthy book designed for older children during the course of several group times to two-year-olds is not developmentally appropriate. A book that is too long for a group of two's to listen to in one sitting should not be used with them at all.

Some books that are fine to read with one or two children are a poor choice to read to a larger group. Choose books for group time carefully. Look for books that:

- ☆ Are large enough for everyone to see
- ☆ Have a simple plot
- ☆ Are short and not too wordy
- ☆ Have colorful and attractive illustrations
- ☆ Have auditory appeal—include sounds of animals or objects
- ☆ Invite participation or repetition, like *Millions of Cats* by Wanda Gag and *Caps for Sale* by Esphyr Slobodkina
- ☆ Avoid sex role stereotypes

I suggest avoiding books that feature popular TV, movie, or cartoon characters. These books rely on the marketing gimmick that children will recognize the characters. Often, the quality of writing is poor, and there really is no story.

ASK YOURSELF:

Do you use books that are developmentally appropriate and have simple, clear illustrations and good stories?

51. Don't hesitate to modify the story to fit your group

YOU TOO CAN BE AN EDITOR

Sometimes I will come upon a book with wonderful illustrations but a plot line that I do not care for. The story may be too long, too complicated, or communicate a message I am not comfortable with. I use it anyway—AFTER I modify it.

HELP!

You can change the vocabulary, content, ending, or message of a story. The library or book publisher police squad will not swoop down into your classroom and hand you a ticket. Seriously, sometimes there are wonderful illustrations but the text is just too wordy for the children's attention span, or children get antsy and you need to end the story in a hurry. Do it. There is nothing worse than torturing you and the children with a story that no one wants to hear.

> Because films and videos cannot be modified and do not allow for teacher-child interaction, their use should be kept to a minimum.

> Needless to say (but I'm going to say it anyway), all material should be carefully previewed before using it.

ASK YOURSELF:

Do you modify stories so that they are developmentally appropriate for your group?

If the children are not interested in what you are doing, do you plow ahead or do you stop and go on to something else?

Do you screen all material before using it?

Try This

Create a story corner where children can sit and tell stories to willing listeners.

Don't always do story time in the same location; occasionally try telling a story outdoors.

Let children listen to a story while lying down with their eyes closed.

Encourage participation at story time by providing instruments for the children to create sound effects.

Read poems, and when possible encourage children to join in the refrain.

At group time listen to a tape of prerecorded sounds normally heard in a house, park, street, or some other location.

Help children to create stories of their own. Gather a few props together, such as a magic wand, scarf, hat, ball, and teaspoon. Discuss the items with the children, and then ask them to make up a story using the props.

Ask your local librarian for the list of recommended books published by the Association for Library Service to Children. The Caldecott Medal is awarded annually to the artist of the most distinguished picture book for children. Selecting Caldecott Medal and Honor books for your book corner is always a good idea.

5

Never Mind the Answer, It's the Question That Matters

Exploring Science Should Be an Adventure

Recently I watched a TV show about the origin of the universe. I was struck by comments made by several of the experts during the program. Walter Lewin, a physicist at MIT, when talking about the existence of black holes, commented, "That is pretty bizarre; that goes totally beyond any imagination."

When discussing recent research into string theory, which works only if there are 10 or more dimensions, Michio Kaku, a physicist from CCNY, stated, "Some say this violates common sense. Why should the universe care about YOUR common sense? We have to go where mathematics and experiments take us."

Young children readily go where observation and experiments take them. They have a wonderful ability to think originally, beyond imagination, and are not fettered by common sense. We must nurture and protect this ability.

Somewhere, something incredible is waiting to be known.

—*Carl Sagan*

52. Ask leading questions that encourage children to think and wonder

MYSTERY

In January we were having our first light snowfall of the year. The snow had started to fall just as we went indoors. The children spent a lot of time looking out the windows and were anxious to go outside at the end of the day. There was snow on the grass, the swing set, and the slide. Jared, an avid tricycle rider, noticed that there was no snow on the blacktop tricycle path. He was pleased because he would still be able to enjoy his favorite activity. I then pointed out that there was no snow by the picnic table (also on blacktop) and said aloud, "I wonder why?" This led children to observe and then speculate about where the snow was or was not accumulating. During the course of that winter we had a lot of good discussions as children observed that snow melted faster on some areas of the playground than on others.

HELP!

I confess that I did know why the snow melted on the blacktop (having absorbed the heat from sunlight the surface was warmer than the grass or slide). Had I declared this fact, some children would have said "Oh" and that would have been the end of that. By my posing a question, and making it a mystery, the children were encouraged to observe and draw some conclusions of their own.

There is a tendency to answer a child's questions too quickly. Asking leading questions is as important as providing facts. Obviously a balance has to be struck, but think carefully before responding to a child. Are you more likely to encourage exploration and observation by not giving an immediate answer? It is a hard new habit for an adult to develop, but the stimulation it provides is very worthwhile.

The most beautiful thing we can experience is the mysterious.
It is the source of all true science.

—Albert Einstein

ASK YOURSELF:

Do you help the children develop observation skills, thinking, and imagination by not answering all questions immediately?

Do you guide and encourage further exploration?

53. Recognize and build on a child's natural curiosity

CATCH A SUNBEAM

One sunny afternoon I was sitting at the art table chatting with one of the children. Several others were looking up on the wall behind me where a rainbow had appeared. It was causing quite a stir. When I turned around to see what was happening, the rainbow disappeared. I turned back to the table only to hear the children start to giggle as the rainbow reappeared. I finally realized that the ring on my finger was acting as a prism, catching the sunbeam and causing a rainbow to appear on the wall. Now that I understood the situation I took advantage of it and playfully wiggled my finger to cause the rainbow to travel all over the wall.

I then gathered up unbreakable (metal) mirrors and some prisms for the children to experiment with. They took them all over the room, trying different positions and angles until they met with success. What a feeling of power to control sunbeams and make them dance about the classroom. We took the materials onto the playground where more discoveries were made. Shadows, shade, as well as angles and beams of light were all examined by the children.

HELP!

Adults should be ready, willing, and able to take advantage of spontaneous events. When children discover a rainbow, icicles, frogs, worms, ladybugs, spider webs, or bird's nests, they will want to know about them right then and there. A flexible, well-prepared teacher will have some basic scientific knowledge and materials on hand to take advantage of the children's natural curiosity.

The art of teaching is the art of assisting discovery.

—Mark Van Doren

ASK YOURSELF:

 Do you build on a child's natural curiosity about a subject, or do you stick to the lesson plan for the day?

54. Provide interesting materials for children to handle, classify, and order

BARGAIN EDUCATIONAL MATERIALS

I enjoy visiting gift shops at museums, zoos, and art galleries almost as much as visiting the places themselves. They can be wonderful to poke around in. Sadly, many of the things I would like to purchase and bring back to the classroom are beyond my budget. But, I have found one item that I can be extravagant about, and buy almost as many as I want. I invest in picture postcards. They can be used in so many different ways.

♦ Classifying (Grouping by common characteristic):

Put all the animals with fur here, and those with feathers there.

Put all the big animals here, and the little ones there.

Put the animals that could live in your house here, and the ones that need to stay outdoors there.

Put all the animals here and all the plants there.

Put all the things that have motors (cars, planes) here, and those that do not (bicycles, wagons) there.

♦ Seriating (Ordering according to a graduated scale or timeline):

Arrange the animals from smallest to largest.

Arrange a tree from seed to sapling to mature tree.

Arrange the buildings from tallest to shortest.

♦ Concentration: Show the children three or four picture postcards. Turn them face down and have the children try to remember where one of the pictures, for example the elephant, is located. To make this more challenging, you can increase the number of cards.

HELP!

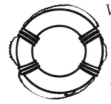

We do not always need to purchase expensive teaching materials. There are many things that children can classify or seriate in our everyday environment. From the very simplest for the young child such as pairing socks or shoes, to classifying or seriating:

- M & M's (Be careful your materials are not eaten up too quickly.)
- Sample color paint cards from hardware stores (Differences can be very subtle.)
- Ribbons of different length, width, and color
- Various sizes of twigs
- Rocks
- Leaves

Be sure all items are large enough so that there is no danger of choking, should a child decide to pop something into her mouth.

By providing matching, classifying, and seriating activities we help children to develop the ability to think analytically and to deal with abstract concepts. These critically important skills are necessary not only for the study of science but also for the study of mathematics.

ASK YOURSELF:

Do you provide different materials for the children to handle, classify, and order?

Do you use many everyday, readily available items, or rely only on the limited number of expensive materials purchased by the school?

55. Help children develop observation and logical reasoning skills

ORDER THE WORLD

I collect seashells. One year I brought a bag full of them into the classroom, dumped them onto the carpet, and posed a question to the children: "Which ones belong together?" The numerous solutions that the children came up with to answer the question were interesting. Some of the groupings that they used were:

- ☆ Big (Daddy) seashells—Little (baby) seashells
- ☆ Dark color seashells—Light color seashells
- ☆ Broken seashells—Good seashells
- ☆ Pretty seashells—Not as pretty (some would say ugly) seashells
- ☆ Smooth seashells—Bumpy seashells

HELP!

In this activity I again provided interesting materials for children to classify and order. However, instead of suggesting the criteria for classifying based on established facts (a bear has fur and a bird has feathers), I asked the children to determine their own groupings. By doing this, I encouraged them to problem solve and arrive at conclusions through observation, a process that is fundamental to science.

> We should respect the children's logic on how to group things. Observing and thinking are more important than getting the right answer. We are teaching a process, not facts.

Even in science, not all groupings are obvious. Mammals live on land (except for whales and dolphins), birds fly (except for the ostrich, penguin, and kiwi), and fish must stay in water (except for mudfish, which can move on land). Children can come up with their own logical, if not sophisticated, groupings, and we should be open minded about them. As penguins, whales, dolphins, and mudfish show, generalizations can go only so far.

> The ability to recognize patterns and groupings is an important skill that can be used to solve problems in both science and mathematics.

ASK YOURSELF:

Do you provide activities that help children develop observation and logical reasoning skills?

Do you encourage the children's use of the scientific process by accepting the children's logic and letting them classify things according to their own ideas, or do you focus on having them learn and parrot facts?

56. Teach some basic principles of physics

SIMPLE TOOLS

During the winter months, when days inside are very long, I do a unit called Simple Tools. In the block corner, I set up a single and a double pulley (which are hung from the ceiling). The children just love loading up the attached basket and giving their favorite toys rides. Somewhere in the course of the activity, the children realize that the double pulley is twice as easy to operate as the single pulley. Because of its ability to lift a much heavier load with the same force as that required for the single pulley, it becomes the favorite.

> The pulleys need to be supervised carefully for safety, just like the workbench and cooking activities.

HELP!

 We can help children understand that we use simple tools based on the principles of physics all through our day:

☆ Wheels—just imagine a supermarket cart, dump truck, or wagon without wheels.

☆ Gears—there are visible gears in eggbeaters and wind up toys.

☆ Levers—we make a lever out of the screwdriver when we use it to pry open a half-used can of paint. The claw end of a hammer, which gives us the strength to remove nails, is another example of a lever. Archimedes, an ancient Greek scientist and mathematician, said that he could lift the earth itself if he just had a long enough lever to do the job.

On the playground, the slide is a perfect place to do physics experiments. Gather up different objects such as paper, crayons, mittens, small blocks, balls, and toy cars for the children to watch go down the slide. Encourage them to observe the varying speeds at which different objects go down the slide.

ASK YOURSELF:

Do you have opportunities available for the children to discover some basic principles of physics?

Do you provide pulleys, levers, and gears for the children to observe and experiment with?

Do you encourage the children to use the slide on the playground for science experiments?

57. Help children explore sound

RAIN MUSIC

Angela was having a great time running in and out of the sprinkler. She was busy running under the water, first with a large plastic bowl and then a pie tin on her head. She called out in delight, "I'm making rain music."

HELP!

Next time you have a heavy rain, instead of listening only to the sound of water in the drainpipe, place upside-down pots, pans, and plastic bowls outdoors near your classroom. Listen to the sounds the raindrops make as they hit on the different surfaces. You can also experiment with other materials. Aluminum foil, plastic, paper, and other materials will each sound a little different when rain falls on them. Instead of an inconvenience, heavy rainfall can be viewed as an opportunity to create rain music.

♦ To encourage the exploration of sound in- and out of doors, I suggest having the following unbreakable items available for the children to experiment with by tapping on with plastic, wooden, and metal spoons:

Wood block	Small cardboard box
Piece of carpet	Sandpaper
Pie tin	Rock
Pot lid	Ball of aluminum foil
Metal triangle (no string handle)	Small tin box
Metal triangle (with string handle)	Plastic bowl
Corrugated cardboard	Milk containers—empty and filled with sand

♦ Have children feel the vibration on a drum as it is struck.

◆ Fill several small boxes or film containers with different materials such as rice, sand, cotton, or beans. Have children shake them and listen. If you fill two boxes with the same kind of material, the children can try to match the sounds.

ASK YOURSELF:

Do you provide materials and opportunities for children to explore sound?

58. Help children discover basic properties of light

MAKE A SHADOW

I fondly remember my childhood Thanksgiving dinners with my relatives and friends gathered close at hand. After dinner, and better than any pumpkin or apple pie, my Uncle Paul would bring the movie projector out of the closet and show us home movies. We sat around watching old movies of people long since gone. When the movies were over my uncle would leave the projector lamp on for a few minutes. What a treat that was! All the children would dance and prance around creating all sorts of shadows on the big screen at the other end of the living room. I guess it was meant to keep us busy while the adults went back to the table for seconds on dessert. I thought it was more fun than any dessert could ever be.

We all know that within 30 seconds of turning on a slide or movie projector there will be several children who can't resist the opportunity to jump up and create shadows. After all, it is a chance to be bigger than life. Rather than fight this natural tendency—even adults usually submit to it—I decided to encourage it at a more opportune time.

HELP!

On a cloudy day, in a poorly lit corner of the room, I set up a projector (a bright flashlight or desk lamp with a focused beam will also work nicely) and the projection screen. I provided various small objects from the room such as toy cars, Legos, and scissors that could be held and manipulated in front of the light. The children had a wonderful time as, in addition to their hands, they held up various objects in front of the beam of light. They discovered how to increase/decrease the size of the shadow by moving the objects closer or farther away from the source of the light. Even the basic fact that no shadow could be created unless the light beam was interrupted was discovered.

Lights can be very hot. Safety and constant supervision are essential.

Translucent color paddles, prisms, magnifying glasses and flashlights should all be available for the children to experiment with.

ASK YOURSELF:

Do you provide opportunities for the children to learn about the basic properties of light?

Do you have translucent color paddles, prisms, magnifying glasses, flashlights, and other items for the children to manipulate and experiment with?

59. Simplify scientific tools for the children to use

IS IT COLD ENOUGH YET?

Once December rolled around and the stores had put up their holiday decorations, the children were constantly asking me if it was going to snow. I would respond, "It has to be cold enough first." In defense against this never-ending question, I devised a way to simplify reading a thermometer so the children could check the temperature on their own. If it was below freezing (32 degrees), they would know it was cold enough for it to snow. I put up two large thermometers on the playground, one in the shade, the other in full sunlight. I created color-coded zones on the thermometers and drew little pictures to help the children begin to understand different temperature ranges and their significance.

Degrees	Color Code	Illustration
100–120	Red	House
80–99	Yellow	Swimsuit
60–79	Orange	Short pants
50–59	Green	Sweater or light jacket
33–49	Blue	Hat and mittens
15–32	White	Snowflake or snowman
0–15	Silver	House

By showing a house at either end of the thermometer, I was indicating that at times it could be too hot or too cold to be outdoors. Either extreme could be unhealthy.

I also made a cardboard thermometer with a movable red elastic strip as the indicator for use in the classroom. It had the same zones and illustrations as the real thermometers outdoors. During the cold days of February, the children enjoyed setting the temperature to 90 and pretending that we could all go swimming.

HELP!

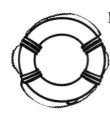

Many scientific tools are much too complex for children to use. However, there are some, like the thermometer, that we can simplify enough for them to use on their own.

ASK YOURSELF:

Do you try to simplify materials, including scientific tools, so the children can use them successfully?

60. Observe and study natural phenomena outdoors

SPLISH SPLASH

Several years ago I visited a nursery school that required each child to keep a raincoat, hat, and boots at the school at all times. The director was a firm believer in exploring the outdoors and wanted the children to be able to play outside regardless of the weather conditions. This approach obviously met with parental approval as the school was always fully enrolled.

HELP!

How many times have you avoided going outdoors because it was too wet? We all know what a few young, enthusiastic puddle-jumpers can do, but there is an opportunity for learning out there. Put on the boots and take advantage of the hands-on learning experiences that a rainy day provides. The power and flow of water is a good subject for children to explore. Observe the flow of water after, or better yet, during a heavy rain. Before going out, speculate with the children. Where do they think the puddles will be? Where will we find the biggest puddle, and why? Can we enlarge or create some puddles of our own? Then give them the opportunity to observe and experiment with the flow of water.

♦ Play with the wind on a windy day—have the children make kites, use streamers or scarves. Blow soap bubbles.

ASK YOURSELF:

Do you encourage observation and scientific exploration outdoors as well as indoors?

Do you have activities and materials ready so you can take advantage of the learning opportunities that rainy and windy days present?

61. Create opportunities for children to observe living things in their natural environment

ANTS

I grew up in New York City, the Bedford-Stuyvesant section of Brooklyn to be exact. There Mother Nature would show her glory in the weeds that struggled to grow in the crack of a broken sidewalk, or the ants crawling on a discarded Popsicle stick left in the gutter. No matter where you are, there will be living things to observe.

Ants provide wonderful observation opportunities. While they always show up at picnics, sometimes they are hard to locate on the playground. At a reasonable distance from the school (I do believe ants belong outdoors), leave snacks for the ants. Salt, sugar, peanut butter (always a favorite), cookie crumbs soaked in soda, and some tiny pieces of fruit or vegetables work well. I would place each snack on a white paper plate or piece of paper that was weighted down so it would not blow away. This provided a good observation area. Sometimes, I would have to add a few extra crumbs on the ground to help alert the ants to the snack. I suggest using only three or four snacks and paper plates at a time. It was interesting to have the children speculate about which snack they thought the ants would be most attracted to—another question to be answered by observation.

HELP!

The young child seems to have an inherent interest in everything. Bugs, worms, plants, rocks, puddles, lint, dust balls, cracks in the wall or floor, all get close and loving inspection. Children have an open mind to the exploration of their environment. We must treasure this attitude, and be careful not to impose the prejudices and fears we have developed as adults. Children's natural sense of wonder helps them find and see the tiniest sorts of treasures in- or out of doors. Some of the best science experiences for the young child are those involving observation.

♦ A bird feeder placed near a classroom window will delight the children even if the only visitors are squirrels.

"Look but don't touch" is an important safety factor when dealing with ants, other insects, or anything you are not thoroughly familiar with, as bites, stings, and allergic reactions can be serious.

ASK YOURSELF:

Do you create opportunities for the children to observe living things in their natural environment?

Do you role-model interest and enthusiasm in observing animals, insects, and plants?

Are you careful not to communicate any negative feelings or fears you may have about worms, spiders, and other creatures?

62. Bring animals, plants, and scientific equipment into your classroom

BILLY GOATS

For a number of years I shared a classroom with a wonderful, enthusiastic teacher. She just never ran out of energy. Mrs. Smiley taught the morning class, and I came in for the afternoon session. I couldn't ask for a better roommate. The classroom was always spotless when she left, and we got along very well.

One day in May, on my way in to work, I decided to cut through the playground to check on our vegetable garden. The last time I had looked, the radishes were almost ready to be harvested and the carrots were doing just fine. As I opened the gate I saw what looked like a small goat eating in the garden that my class had planted. I really couldn't believe my eyes, but after a few seconds (I knew I hadn't had anything to drink lately) I accepted what my eyes were telling me and raced over to protect my class garden. I shooed the goat away. As I stepped in some foreign matter that had been deposited near the garden, courtesy of the goat, I posted myself like a human scarecrow trying to fend off this intruder. The morning class came out on the playground for dismissal, and Mrs. Smiley was shocked to see what the goat had done. She was very sorry and apologized at length. Meantime the children wanted to pet the goat and kept him busy scurrying about the yard. At least he was no longer eating my radishes.

After the children left, a young man in a pickup truck came to retrieve the goat and take him back to the farm. Catching the goat took the coordinated effort of one farm hand, two teachers, and several college students who happened to walk by and decided to join in what looked like a fun activity. Goats are very fast, agile animals. It was quite a sight to behold. All these adults chasing around after one small, but very fast goat, who still insisted on making a few passes through what was left of our class garden. Finally, after about 15 minutes, the farm hand made a flying tackle and caught the goat. He really would have made a fine football player!

HELP!

Arrange for visitors to come to the classroom who bring in animals, plants, scientific equipment, and materials for the children to observe and handle—for example, staff from a nature center, firefighters, paramedics, nurses, musicians, amateur rock collectors, scuba divers, and spelunkers. See if you can borrow some of their equipment so the children can examine it at their leisure in the classroom.

Before inviting animal guests you should think about your own level of expertise. Do you know enough to provide a safe environment for the children as well as the guest goat, snake, or whatever? Are the facilities you will provide appropriate for the animal? Will an expert be there to supervise if something unplanned occurs?

ASK YOURSELF:

Do you invite guests to bring in authentic scientific equipment for the children to see and, when appropriate, use?

Do you try to arrange for living things to be brought into the classroom?

Do you make appropriate arrangements for the safety of all?

63. Set up science experiments

WATER AND ICE

One particularly cold winter everything seemed to turn to ice. I decided to take advantage of this and do some experimenting with water and ice. The children and I filled (to the brim) several empty gallon plastic milk jugs with water. We put one in the classroom (for comparison) and left a few on the playground overnight. When water freezes and turns to ice, it expands in volume and this can have dramatic results. Some of the containers that had been left outdoors overnight split open. One container had a loosely fastened cap, and the ice pushed straight up through the spout. The cap was now perched on top of a column of ice. Speculation and discussion about the power of ice, and what had happened and why, was spirited. We filled containers throughout the winter months and well into the spring. When the children arrived at school, they enjoyed checking on the status of our experiment.

This was such a rewarding activity that I did it again for the next several winters, but alas the weather was quite mild and I did not get the same dramatic results. Children wondered why I was bothering when nothing seemed to happen.

Not all experiments work as planned. Observing and speculating are good activities whether the experiment works as planned or not.

HELP!

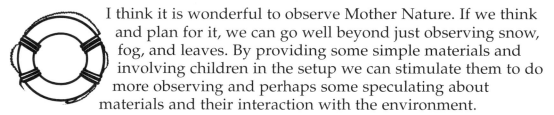 I think it is wonderful to observe Mother Nature. If we think and plan for it, we can go well beyond just observing snow, fog, and leaves. By providing some simple materials and involving children in the setup we can stimulate them to do more observing and perhaps some speculating about materials and their interaction with the environment.

Here are a few additional good observation activities that almost always work. Remember, nothing in life is guaranteed:

♦ To observe the effect temperature has on snow, try partially filling several cups with snow (or ice if snow is not available) and placing them in various locations, such as indoors near and away from heat and outdoors in shady and sunny areas. Because of the different temperatures in each location they should melt and turn to liquid at different rates (but don't spoil it by telling that to the children before you begin).

♦ In the spring, when we start to get long sunny days, tape a few pieces of black construction paper to a table in the sun on the playground. Ask the children to gather up a few small toys and place them on the paper. (Children in my classes have selected everything from blocks of different shapes to scissors, large pegs, toy cars, and the frying pan from the housekeeping corner.) Depending on the intensity of the sun, this can provide some interesting effects. The sun will bleach out the area around the toys, and when the toys are removed their silhouettes will appear on the paper.

♦ Place plants near windows and observe how, over time, leaves turn toward the source of light.

♦ Use cooking to observe the effects of heat on different foods. You can make potatoes soft, raw eggs hard, liquid pudding creamy, and the all time-favorite, cupcakes grow big in the oven.

♦ In the winter it is easy to observe the effects of static electricity. Hair stands on end when a sweater is removed. One can also rub a balloon on a sweater and then have it stick to clothing.

♦ Observe the effect of magnets on different materials.

Remember to involve the children when setting up experiments.

ASK YOURSELF:

Do you set up science experiments for the children to observe and think about?

Do you involve the children in helping to set up experiments in and out of the classroom?

64. Teach respect and care for the environment

MIKEY THE GOLDFISH

I took my class on a trip to a pet store. We purchased a goldfish that the children named Mikey. The children took the responsibility of caring for Mikey very seriously. They obviously did an excellent job since Mikey lived for over five years.

HELP!

To help teach care and respect for the environment and all living things, provide opportunities for children to properly care for plants and animals.

♦ Take a trip to a pet store or plant and garden nursery, and bring back a living thing for the children to care for.

> Select plants carefully. Some are poisonous.

♦ Set up a signup sheet so the class pet can visit the children's homes over holidays and long weekends.

ASK YOURSELF:

Do you provide opportunities for the children to care for living things?

Is teaching respect and care for the environment part of your curriculum?

Try This

Go on listening, smelling, and touching walks in- and out of doors.

Experiment with the sense of smell. Place cotton balls in small containers. Put some perfume, vanilla, lemon juice, or cinnamon on each cotton ball. Have children match the scents.

Set up a taste table. Have things that taste salty, sweet, and sour.

Set up a feely box. Have a box with an opening just large enough for the child's hand to fit in. Place objects in it and have a child reach in and, without looking, talk about how an object feels.

Talk about texture and observe what happens when you add items like salt, sand, or rice to finger paint or shaving cream.

Notice the different textures of tree bark, leaves, plants, soil, and other materials.

When planting a garden choose radishes and carrots as they grow very quickly and require minimal care. Sunflowers grow very high and usually dwarf the children by the end of summer.

Plant lima beans in clear plastic cups and observe the roots as they grow.

Start a rock collection. Ask the children to bring in interesting rocks that they have found.

Set up a simple sundial outside. A stick in the ground will do. Notice where the shadow is at different times of the day.

Use chalk to trace a child's shadow on the ground. Do this at different times of the day. Notice how the size of the shadow changes depending on the time of day.

On rainy days, ask the children to sprinkle dry tempera paint on a piece of paper and then place it out in the rain. Watching the effect of raindrops on the paint (or even on a blank piece of construction paper) is another great opportunity to practice observation skills.

At the water table, offer an opportunity to mix colors. Use food color to prepare gallon jugs of red, blue, and yellow. Give the children small cups of these colors and plastic eyedroppers. A clear plastic cup or muffin tin can be used for their experimenting.

6

"How Many Cookies Do You Want?"

Teaching Mathematics That Is Relevant to Young Children

Teaching mathematics involves more than counting to 100 and being able to read numbers. Concepts such as bigger, smaller, more or less, and the ability to compare amounts, organize information, and think logically are all part of mathematics. When children start to truly understand numbers and what they represent, they become empowered. Decisions and understanding about all aspects of their daily activities are enhanced. If you think about it, we would be stymied if we couldn't use numbers and mathematical concepts to communicate. I'm sure you could add to the following examples:

You can have 10 pushes on the swing.

Would you like a half cup of juice?

You have to wait two turns before you can use the bike.

How many cookies would you like?

Cleanup time is in five minutes.

We only have three fire engines, and so we have to share.

133

Would you like half of my play dough?

Are you ready to go down the slide? When I count to three—1, 2, 3!

Get your coat on before I count to three—1, 2, 2¼, 2½, 3.

Stir the batter six times, and then it is Kyle's turn.

Three more pails of water and the water table will be full.

We need to line up by two's.

The recipe says "two cups of sugar."

Mathematical learning should take place all day long. Provide a rich environment for the children to explore, and be ready to engage them in mathematics whenever the opportunity presents itself.

65. Help children understand one-to-one correspondence

I CAN COUNT

Four-year-old Wayne rushed into the classroom. "Guess what?" he said. "I can count to twenty, Grandpa taught me. You want to hear?" Of course I did. Wayne then began, saying the numbers very quickly, "One, two, three, four, five, six, seven, eight, nine, ten, eleventeen, tweleveteen, thirteen, fourteen, fifteen, sixteen, septeen, eighteen, nineteen, twentyteen." When he finished he had a big grin on his face, and he just beamed with pride.

HELP!

Children just love to rote count (saying the numbers in order). I have spent many a happy moment patiently listening to children go all the way to 100. However, just because they can recite numbers does not indicate they understand what they mean. To help children learn what numbers represent, have them count objects. Tell them to touch each object as they say a number. Since they are so familiar with rote counting, frequently their mouths (saying the number out loud) will move much faster than their hands. You will probably need to remind the children to slow down and say a number only when their hand touches an object. This approach will help them to grasp the concept of one-to-one correspondence. Mathematics has to start on a firm base of tactile (touching) experiences. As children mature they will be able to count in their heads and not have to touch the objects. Moving to that step too quickly will cause them to be less sure of themselves and their understanding of mathematics.

Touching and counting objects outside of the classroom can include steps, nails on a fence, or trees on the playground. When the child no longer needs to touch objects, you can move on to such interesting things as counting cars, trucks, worms, and birds.

One and one make two. That's great. What's a two?

—Bill Cosby

ASK YOURSELF:

Do you respect the child's need to touch and handle materials?

Are interesting materials (seashells, leaves, raisins, toys) provided for counting?

66. Provide meaningful mathematical experiences

HOW MANY CRACKERS?

One day, at snack time, I asked each child in turn, "How many crackers do you want?" Most children said three or four. It had been my experience that children usually ask for the same number as their age. Kenesha was watching me very carefully as I responded to each child's request. When I finally got to Kenesha and asked her how many crackers she wanted, she smiled very broadly and with a twinkle in her eye said in a bold voice, "I want seven crackers." I acknowledged her request and carefully counted out the crackers. Fortunately for me I had only two more children at the table, and they both requested three crackers. Needless to say, many of the children noticed how many crackers Kenesha was given.

HELP!

 Here was a situation where a child clearly understood that seven was more than three or four, and was able to use that knowledge to her benefit. Try to provide situations where counting is not just an exercise but has real meaning for the child. Counting carrot sticks, pretzels, or spoonfuls of raisins, which the children know they are going to consume, will get the undivided attention of most youngsters. When they truly learn the meaning of the numbers, there may have to be some limits—such as three to five carrot sticks today. Giving the children the power to determine how many pieces of food they can take (within reasonable guidelines) is a meaningful way to teach mathematics.

♦ On the subject of food, have children make half or quarter sandwiches to eat.

Is it not joy to use knowledge you have gained?

—Confucius

ASK YOURSELF:

Do you provide meaningful mathematical experiences for the children?

67. Make mathematics an integral part of classroom activities

ELECTION DAY

Living just inside the beltway in the Washington, D.C., area meant that Election Day was extra special. One year I decided to try to have an election in our four-year-old classroom. Rather than voting for personalities, we were going to vote for which book would be read at story time. The choices were *Caps for Sale* or *Whistle for Willie*. I prepared simple ballots. On a single sheet of paper I had an illustration to represent each of the books. The children were told to color in the picture of the book they wanted read later that day. I was pleasantly surprised at how seriously the children took making this decision. During free play those who wanted to vote, colored in their choice. Ballots were collected in a shoe box. (I hope they never sell shoes in plastic bags!) At the end of free play we gathered on the carpet and counted the ballots. Interest was so high that I decided to post the ballots on a wall so the children could count them during the course of the day. I lined up the ballots in two straight lines so that it was clearly visible which story had gotten more votes. *Whistle for Willie* was declared the winner!

HELP!

This was a good activity, and like so many things we do with young children, multiple subjects were touched on. Reading, small motor control, mathematics, vocabulary, and the voting process itself were explored. Displaying the objects to be counted (in this case the ballots), so that they are carefully lined up and the children can visually see which group is larger, is something we should try to do whenever the counting of two or more sets is involved. If possible, try to line the items up from left to right, and then immediately under that form another line of objects for easy comparison. One line will be longer than the other, and visually help the children understand that the higher number represents more.

> Equal spacing and size of objects is important when comparing sets. Jean Piaget, the noted child psychologist, would remind us that three spread-out coins would appear to be more to a young child than five similar coins that had been scrunched together.

ASK YOURSELF:

Do you try to use mathematics as an integral part of classroom activities?

Do you incorporate visual clues, such as the size of a group, to help children grasp number concepts?

68. Turn the calendar into a mathematical learning tool

WHEN ARE WE GOING TO THE FIRE STATION?

I tried to keep the calendar interesting and meaningful to the children. At the beginning of each month, I would post symbols on the calendar to represent significant dates. For example, if Ricky was going to turn four on the 20th, on a small piece of paper I would draw a picture of a cake with "Ricky" written on it. I would tape the piece of paper to the location on the calendar that coincided with his birthday. I did the same thing for class trips, special events, and holidays. I even posted little houses for Saturday and Sunday when we stayed at home and did not go to school.

HELP!

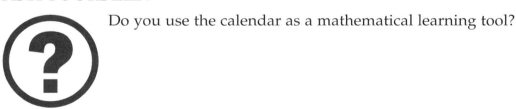

Children would invariably ask, "How long until my birthday?" or "When will we go on our trip?" This now became a counting experience. We would go over to the calendar and count days (represented by the empty boxes) until the special event. Many children caught on to the idea and would do this without the help of an adult. They were in fact learning to use a calendar.

ASK YOURSELF:

Do you use the calendar as a mathematical learning tool?

69. Create simple graphs

CLOUDY WITH A CHANCE OF SHOWERS

"What is the weather today?" is one of the most frequently asked questions at group time. I think it is a great question for several reasons. It encourages observation, is easy for children to answer, and the weather changes. We can observe that it is raining at 10 a.m., and then have clear sunny skies by 2 p.m. Another golden opportunity buried in this question is the chance to track the weather for the month or even longer.

HELP!

When dealing with children who are so young that any number greater than five is not meaningful, I use the calendar in the following way. I prepare pre-cut symbols to represent the weather—for example, sun, cloud, umbrella, and snowman. Each day during group time we observe the weather and then tape on the appropriate symbol in the little square where the number is usually written. At the end of the month we clear off the old symbols, re-label the name of the month, and start all over again.

Keeping track of the weather using symbols stimulates good conversations about how many sunny days we have had this month, or how few rainy days. The concept of more/less is visually presented to the children. They can readily see, for example, that we had a lot more suns than snowmen. Those interested may want to count how many rainy days we have had as compared to snowy days. On Monday, be sure to post the weather for the past weekend so that the tally for the month is correct.

In older classes, where you write in the dates on the calendar, you can create a simple bar graph for each month using weather symbols. On a 9-by-12-inch piece of paper use separate lines for Cloudy, Rainy, Snowy, and Sunny. Each day, draw on the graph an umbrella, a sun, or whatever is appropriate for that day. Again, as the month goes on you can talk about how many suns there are, compared to umbrellas—or other symbols. If space permits, you can post the graphs for all the months on a wall at the children's eye level. Now the children can, on their own, tally up how many snowy days we have had so far this year, or decide which month had more rainy days, or make any other comparisons they care to. This simple graphing activity stimulates mathematical discussions. One year, I had some children who decided they wanted to know how many rainy days we had had that year, and then proceeded to count all the umbrellas I had drawn for the months of September through May. The children help create the weather graph, watch it grow, and are therefore drawn to it.

> If you use special shapes (leaves in September, pumpkins in October, turkeys in November, etc.) on which you write the correct date, do not throw them away at the end of the month. Children enjoy playing with them, and some will recreate the sequence of dates for themselves.

ASK YOURSELF:

Do you create simple graphs with the children?

Do you display graphs at the children's eye level in the room?

70. Develop activities that involve pattern recognition

DRUM BEATS

A popular story I told to my four-year-old class led to an interesting mathematical learning opportunity. The story is about a boy who goes out in the woods. He has a drum that he can beat on to send coded messages to his father. The boy gets lost and is in danger when a bear gets too close for comfort. The boy frantically beats a message to his father, and the father in turn beats back a message saying he is on the way. Of course there is a happy ending with father and son safely reunited.

Later in the week we made drums out of coffee cans and oatmeal boxes. I was delighted when Susan and Mary started recreating the story. Susan went to the block corner and started tapping out a message. Mary at the other end of the room used her drum to respond.

HELP!

I made sure those drums were available during free play for the next few weeks. The re-enactment of the story expanded and soon the children were copying drum beat patterns back and forth. The varieties are endless, two quick taps, one long, four loud beats, two soft ones, and so on. The children were inventing all kinds of codes, and in the process of playing their games they were counting drumbeats and remembering sequence as well. It turned out to be a good mathematical learning experience.

Counting, sequencing, and pattern recognition can also be taught by playing games. For example, you can clap your hands in a particular pattern, such as two fast followed by two slow, or tap different parts of your body, such as one tap on the nose followed by two taps on the leg. Then ask the children to match your pattern. The hardest part for the children is being patient enough to wait to observe your pattern before they try to copy it. Of course, the children should have an opportunity to challenge the adult and be able to originate patterns of their own. I caution you that this can get very complex.

Helping children to develop the ability to create and recognize patterns involving counting and sequencing builds on the teaching of the prior chapter in which children were introduced to classifying, matching, and seriating activities.

ASK YOURSELF:

Do you expose children to activities that involve counting, sequencing, and pattern recognition?

71. Use measuring tools to create mathematical learning opportunities

HOW LONG IS YOUR ARM?

One of the more popular activities in my class was hooking plastic links together to form long chains that the children then used as necklaces or bracelets. On one occasion I had the yardstick out to measure some paper for a mural. I offered to measure one of the chains to see just how long it was. What a great response I got. All of the children wanted to know exactly how long their chain was. We carefully lined them up next to the yardstick and measured. Soon there was heated competition among the children to create the longest chain. Fortunately, in the interest of making the chain as long as we possibly could, the competitors decided to combine each of their portions into one giant chain. The final product was longer than the classroom and reached out into the hallway. It was a wonderful cooperative effort. Interest in the exact length of the chain was intense.

HELP!

 I decided to capitalize on this interest in measuring and brought a few 12-inch rulers into the room. We measured toy cars, blocks, crayons, anything that wasn't nailed down. Some of the children were even starting to guess at just how long an item might be, or who had the longer pencil. We also had fun when we started to measure hair, fingers, arms, and other parts of our bodies. Once again, using real tools to answer real questions became a teaching opportunity.

♦ Don't forget that we can also measure liquids and sand, rice, and other materials. The water table and sandbox should have measuring cups, spoons, and containers of different sizes for the children to experiment with.

♦ Scales and simple balances should be available for the children to use.

ASK YOURSELF:

Do you build on the interest of the children to create mathematical learning opportunities?

Are there rulers, scales, spoons, cups, and containers of varying sizes available for the children to use?

72. Create games and activities involving mathematics

MATH AS A SOURCE OF PLEASURE

When I was growing up, all the boys in my neighborhood were well versed in the most recent statistics of the Brooklyn Dodgers baseball team. While my brother showed no interest or particular talent in mathematics as an academic subject, he was a whiz at doing percentages. In the days before pocket calculators, he would sit in front of the TV set with a stack of paper and a pen doing mathematical calculations after every hit, home run, error, and strikeout that occurred during the course of a game. To me it looked like an endless homework assignment. To my brother it was a compelling interest and source of pleasure.

HELP!

Math can be fun. There are many games children can play that involve number recognition, counting, addition, subtraction, and fractions. Modifying the materials used in these games to ensure that they do not frustrate the children is the key to success. Playing cards and dice, which are easy to modify, are good materials to use to teach and reinforce mathematical concepts.

♦ The card game "War" is based on the idea that the larger number on the face of the card wins over the smaller number. It is a very simple game and excellent for teaching counting and the concept of more/less. To make the game practical for young children, you need to stack the deck. If you feel the children are comfortable and reasonably familiar with recognizing and counting the numbers from one to five, then those are the only cards that you should use. Remove any cards with higher numbers as well as the picture cards. By removing the other cards, you limit the game to the numbers the children can work with effectively. By controlling the deck you can make the game simpler or more challenging, depending on the children's needs.

♦ Children enjoy tossing dice. By creating your own die, you can challenge, but not overwhelm the children. Use a cardboard square box about four by four inches. Cover it with white paper and then paint on the number of dots that you think will challenge but not frustrate the children. It can be kept as simple as having only three dots as the maximum. Just putting a die on the table with a few plastic chips creates a simple counting game. A child rolls the die and gets to keep the corresponding number of chips. When all the chips are gone the game is over, and we can start again if the children want to. Some players may choose to count up all the chips they have collected, and that is a good way to take the activity to a more challenging level.

Be creative; do not restrict the use of dice to numbers alone. Letters, colors, and shapes can also be used to create developmentally appropriate games.

ASK YOURSELF:

Do you provide games and activities that involve counting and number recognition?

Do you modify materials to challenge but not frustrate the children?

Are more advanced mathematical opportunities provided to those children who are ready for them?

73. Provide opportunities for children to make estimates

GUESS HOW MANY

Irene brought an opened can of tennis balls to school, a present she had received from her aunt. At group time she proudly showed it to the class. I asked the children, "How many tennis balls do you think are in the can?" The children answered my question with everything from a shrug of the shoulders to "a hundred, hundred." Naturally we had to solve this mystery. Irene took the lid off the can and let the balls roll onto the rug. We counted two tennis balls.

HELP!

Providing opportunities for children to gain an understanding of what constitutes a reasonable estimate plays an important role in developing their mathematical abilities, and it is fun to do!

Fill a large plastic fish bowl with objects, for example, tennis balls, golf balls, blocks, puzzle pieces, rocks, mittens, socks, crayons, or pencils. Use only one set of objects at a time. Choose the size and number of objects that will challenge but not frustrate the children. After the children have had enough time to look things over carefully and guess at the quantity, count the items by removing them one at a time. This also provides a good opportunity to reinforce one-to-one correspondence. With older children you can fill the fish bowl with large items and then repeat the activity with a set of similar smaller items, for example, tennis balls and then golf balls, or vice versa.

♦ There are many materials we can use to encourage children to estimate quantities. For example:

Flowers in a vase

Dishes or bowls in a stack

Soccer balls in a pillow case

Blocks in a basket

♦ We can ask the children to estimate:

How many cups of water it will take to fill a bottle

How many crayons will fit in a box

How many books will fit on a shelf

How many cups of sand it will take to fill a pail

♦ Encourage the children to make measurement estimates, such as the length of their fingers, the width of a table or the number of steps it takes to cross the playground.

ASK YOURSELF:

Do you provide opportunities for the children to develop the skill to make reasonable estimates?

74. Use flannel board number songs to teach mathematical concepts

HOW DO YOU LIKE TO MAKE THREE?

I enjoy doing flannel board number songs. The children who are able to read numbers or are ready for addition and subtraction problems can be challenged, while those who just enjoy a good song are being entertained. I have created a set of four-by-six index cards with the numbers 1–10 written on individual cards. I also include a card for zero as well. When I have five ducks on the flannel board I show the index card with the appropriate corresponding number.

HELP!

To keep this from becoming just a passive form of entertainment, I try to encourage the children to participate by challenging them. I will sometimes hold up the incorrect number on the index card, and of course, the children just love setting me straight. They can't wait for me to goof again. It is just so satisfying to correct an adult that I get their undivided attention.

Sometimes, I will hold up the fingers of both my hands to show how I like to make the number three. I use two fingers from my right hand, plus one from my left hand. When I move them close together I make three. Sometimes I choose to use three fingers from one hand only. Then I ask the children, "How do you like to make the number three?" The children get very serious about making this choice and concentrate hard on their fingers. Of course, as their skill increases, using additional fingers to make the various combinations of four, five, or higher numbers is even more challenging.

♦ Another concept that can be taught with a flannel board number song is that of "more or less." Are there more ducks at home, or over the mountain? Are there more frogs in the pool, or on the log? Carefully lining up the flannel board figures should make this visually easy for the children to determine. The answer to the more-or-less question will change as the song progresses. Counting the flannel board figures will help reinforce the concept. Four frogs on the log are more than one in the pool—illustrating the fact that four is more than one.

◆ Flannel board songs also present opportunities to use ordinal numbers and teach directional words. For example, the first duck to go over the mountain is followed by the second duck. Concepts such as up/down, front/back, and over/under are easily illustrated with flannel board figures.

Always use correct mathematical vocabulary. For example, the set of apples on the tree is greater than the set of apples on the ground.

ASK YOURSELF:

Do you use flannel board number songs or other entertaining ways to engage the children in mathematics?

Are mathematical concepts and vocabulary, such as set, more/less, equal, big, bigger, biggest, first and second, used throughout the day?

75. Encourage activities that explore mathematical relationships and geometry

BUMPY ROADS

Four-year-old Hy was a block builder extraordinaire. He spent most of his time in the block corner and delighted in using every block shape on the shelf. One day I brought in some small plastic cars, and he naturally set out to build a highway. It was a major undertaking and included bridges, tunnels, steep inclines, and tollbooths. When Hy was almost done he was faced with the problem of how to use the semicircle and triangle blocks. He experimented with using the shapes as decorations for the tollbooths as he usually did with castles, but rejected that idea. He then hit on a very creative solution. Hy decided to use the semicircles and triangles to build a bumpy road. The semicircles created round bumps and the triangles sharp pointy bumps. The children just loved this new road and lined up for turns to use it.

HELP!

Blocks are a wonderful experimental geometric playground. By handling and using different shaped blocks, children are exposed to basic geometric principles such as two semicircles can make a circle, or triangles when placed together can become squares or rectangles. Mathematical relationships and ratios are also discovered when the child realizes that two half-unit-size blocks equal one unit-size block.

> Parents often fret that their children are just playing with blocks and not learning anything. We need to help them appreciate just how much thinking, planning, and mathematical learning are involved in block-building play.

ASK YOURSELF:

Do you encourage children to play with blocks?

Is the supply generous and are they shelved according to their shape and size?

Do you provide materials such as geo boards so children can discover mathematical relationships and explore basic geometric shapes?

Try This

Role model and show interest in counting objects:
* ☆ I wonder how many stairs we have to go down to get to the basement?
* ☆ How many paces to the door, wall, gate?
* ☆ How many leaves can you collect?
* ☆ How many buttons are on your shirt today?
* ☆ How many balls do we have in our room?
* ☆ How many balls are there in the room across the hall?
* ☆ How many red crayons do we have?
* ☆ How many books are on this shelf?
* ☆ How many napkins do we need for snack?

Create games using cards and dice:
* ☆ Have small cars numbered 1–5, and box garages also numbered 1–5. Ask the children to park the cars in the correct garage. Or have them toss a die to determine which car to park.
* ☆ Arrange an area on the other side of the room to which the children can bring things. Have a child toss a die to determine how many objects to carry. You can use small blocks, crayons, dolls, or other objects.
* ☆ Organize a treasure hunt. Give a child a card with a shape, for example, a circle. Then ask him to collect a set of things in the classroom that match that shape.

Create graphs to track things of interest:
* ☆ Number of children in class each day
* ☆ Number of times we drank apple juice, grape juice, or milk
* ☆ Number of times we had snow, rain, extreme cold, or heat and could not go outdoors
* ☆ Number of children wearing something red, blue, green, or another color
* ☆ Height of each child

In the middle of the table put a plastic tub that contains different colored pegs. Give each child a small peg-board. Starting at the simplest level, pick two blue pegs and put them in the middle of your peg-board, side by side. Ask the children to match your pattern. After a few successful matches, take the game to the next level. Create a pattern, show it to the children and encourage them to look hard while you slowly count to three. Then with some drama, like a magician performing a trick, cover up your peg-board. Ask the children to try to remember the pattern and to recreate it on their peg-boards. After giving them enough time, uncover your peg-board and ask them to check to see if they have a match. After the children have several successful matches you can increase the complexity of the game by adding a third peg or varying the colors. Eventually, with some children, you can use as many as five pegs of different colors. This activity can be made even more complex by putting pegs in both vertically and horizontally. Playing this simple game requires great concentration. Children are asked to recall number of pegs used, color, sequence, and direction. You can also ask the children to create a pattern for you to match. Having them check to see if you got it right is another way to challenge them.

Establish a color or shape sequence for the calendar, for example, a square on Monday, followed by a circle on Tuesday and a triangle on Wednesday. Thursday you can start the pattern again.

Make number signs:
  ☆ License plates for the tricycles and wagons
  ☆ Numbered parking spaces

Collect large plastic lids and caps for the children to match and sort.

7

Creativity Is an Attitude, Not an Art Project

Opening Your Mind to Children's Creativity

Some teachers plan what they call an open-ended art project once or twice a week and think they are fostering creativity. While this is good, it is only a starting point. Creativity is not and should not be limited to art. The outstanding musician, writer, teacher, engineer, architect, scientist, athlete, inventor, business leader, and chef all have at least one thing in common. They are willing to look at the world with fresh eyes, to step beyond the way things have always been done and dare to imagine how they can be done differently. This is the very core of creativity. We must reach beyond the standard music and art activities to nurture the creative thinkers of tomorrow so that they will be able to think out of the box.

Imagination is more important than knowledge. Knowledge is limited. Imagination encircles the world.

—Albert Einstein

155

76. Use props to stimulate creative thinking

MIND OVER MATTER

I found a box of tongue depressors in the closet and decided to use them during group time to stimulate creative thought. Holding a tongue depressor in my hand, I asked the children to tell me what they could do with it. The following are just some of their responses:

- ✰ You could hide it
- ✰ Make a puppet
- ✰ Hit a drum
- ✰ Make Popsicles!
- ✰ Scratch your arm
- ✰ Eat applesauce
- ✰ Dig a hole
- ✰ Stir paint
- ✰ Put it in the fire
- ✰ Make Pudding Pops!
- ✰ Cut a cake

Clearly some of the children were hungry and ready for snack time.

HELP!

When trying to foster creative thought, start by talking about things that the children can see and touch. Objects like a tongue depressor, a brick, a scarf, or any other concrete object that the children can handle will work well. If at first all you get from the children are blank looks, shoulder shrugs, and "I don't know" responses, you can try to stimulate discussion by manipulating the object or offering one or two suggestions of your own. Be sure you keep things positive and make this a fun activity for the children. Use phrases like, "Yes that's a good idea, I bet we can think of even more things we could do." "Just listen to all the wonderful different ideas we have; this is exciting." What is most important is accepting their ideas and then encouraging them to think again and again, seeking more and more responses.

ASK YOURSELF:

Do you use props to help children think creatively?

Do you help children understand that there can be many good answers to a single question?

Do you make specific lesson plans to stimulate creative thinking?

77. When you ask open-ended questions, value the children's responses

READ MY MIND

Ms. Quiz taught the four-year-old class. One day in October, when the leaves had started to fall, she asked the children, "What is happening outside?" (A good, thought-provoking, open-ended question.) Some eager beaver called out "Cars." Others called out dogs, cats, and someone guessed clouds. For each response, Ms. Quiz would unenthusiastically say, "Uh-huh" or maybe "Yes"—but it was clear the children's answers were not what she wanted to hear. In desperation she invited the class to look out the window with her. After gathering at the window the cycle of wild guessing began again. Grass, birds, Thanksgiving, fence, people, and cars were all tried. It was obvious the children did not have a clue, but if they kept on guessing wildly, and did not mind the subtle put down of an "Uh-huh" response from the teacher, maybe someone would get lucky. I felt as though Ms. Quiz was really playing READ MY MIND. Finally a child got lucky and put everyone out of their misery by calling out "Leaves." The teacher beamed with approval; at last she had the CORRECT answer. She then pulled a yellow leaf out of a bag and discussed the signs of fall with the children.

HELP!

The wild guessing that goes on when children are asked to read an adult's mind and give the one "correct" response can have a negative impact. When you ask an open-ended question, you should accept and value the children's responses. Children understand the difference between an "Uh-huh" response and an enthusiastic, "That's right! Good for you." We should use discussion times to encourage children to think, not guess. Consider for a moment the thinking that can be stimulated with the following questions:

- ✿ What would you do if an elephant walked into the room right now?
- ✿ What do you think the birds talk about?
- ✿ Where is the squirrel going?
- ✿ Let's pretend there is a magic place you can visit; what would it be like?

✾ Can you imagine what it would be like if we never had rain?

✾ What would you like to talk about?

To encourage the children to think creatively, try starting discussions with "let's pretend," "can you imagine," or "what if."

Wisdom begins in wonder.

—Socrates

ASK YOURSELF:

Do you ask open-ended questions?

Do you respect the children's ideas and encourage the use of imaginative thought, or are you just looking for the one correct answer?

78. Provide open-ended materials

BOREDOM, THE MOTHER OF INVENTION

Recently I was lucky enough to visit Cambodia. It is a beautiful place with friendly, gracious people who are struggling to rebuild their country after many years of warfare. Children, who are so poor that they have no souvenirs or postcards to sell, try to earn a little money by fanning hot, tired tourists as they climb over the ruins of ancient temples.

We had some extra time and went to one of the temples off the beaten path. There was an eerie silence as we explored the ruins. After a while, I heard a number of boisterous children. Intrigued, I followed the sounds. I came upon a group of young boys that I guessed were about six to eight years old. They were very absorbed in a game and did not notice my presence. The game was fairly simple—take the thongs (flip flops) off your feet and throw them to a particular location. It was only when I got a little closer that I realized the object of throwing the thong was to dislodge a rubber band from a circle drawn in the sand. What fun they were having. Excitement! Cheering! Victory! And all this was because of a little imagination, thongs, and a rubber band. When I thought about children back home, many of whom think you can't play soccer unless you have expensive official shoes, a regulation ball, and the proper field, I felt we were the poorer nation of the two.

HELP!

At what point does a rich, fully equipped environment become one that stifles imagination? Surely there must be some reasonable middle ground between using the shoes off your feet as toys and children who sit glassy-eyed, pressing buttons, waiting for things to entertain them. I am a true believer that sometimes more is less. We should not ask children to create in a vacuum; they need stimulation and some basic materials. But let's not fall into the trap of thinking that we must have a perfectly equipped up-to-the-technological-moment environment in order to have children thrive and create.

The less specific the materials are, like blocks, the more imagination the child can use. A block can be the start of an airport, house, road, bed, kitchen, or rocket ship. A fire engine is always a fire engine unless you have very free-thinking young children who are willing to assert themselves over the material and make it respond to their will.

ASK YOURSELF:

Do you provide open-ended materials, such as blocks, so that the children are encouraged to use their imagination when playing?

79. Encourage children to use materials in unconventional ways

ONE RIGHT WAY

Near the art corner, I had a cabinet with various materials for the children to use. One day Vijay noticed a stack of brown paper sandwich bags in the cabinet. He grabbed a handful of them and went over to the block area. There he proceeded to use the bags in an interesting fashion. He laid them down very neatly, end to end, and then he got a few cars to play with. I realized he had created a highway out of paper bags. While this was not the intended purpose for these bags, I decided it was a unique and positive use of the material. After all, if I could use toilet paper rolls for musical instruments (kazoos and shakers), why couldn't Vijay use paper bags for a highway?

HELP!

Fostering creativity means accepting new ways of using materials or doing things. It is amazing what children can create with common household items in a supportive environment.

We should also think about this outdoors. One year I collected milk cartons and then just left them in a large box outside. The children used the cartons to make everything from big shoes to walk in, to obstacles to jump over. They made interesting designs by dragging the cartons in the sandbox, and they also used them as shovels and as building blocks.

♦ Just imagine what other stimulating and creative play would be encouraged if we occasionally provided children with paper plates, scarves, or table cloths with no instructions as to their proper use.

♦ Large boxes in- or out of doors are open invitations to a child's creativity. They can become airplanes, rocket ships, homes, caves, trucks, or anything else that the children want to imagine.

As always, safety must be carefully considered before introducing any materials.

ASK YOURSELF:

Do you encourage children to use materials in unconventional ways?

Do you provide materials that stimulate creativity and imaginative play in the classroom and on the playground?

80. Limit the use of worksheets and patterns

"CREATIVE COLORING BOOK" IS AN OXYMORON

A teacher I know used to joke that she was going to publish a coloring book that fostered creativity. It would have a very colorful cover and inside there would be 20 completely blank pages.

HELP!

 Coloring books and teacher-prepared worksheets and patterns have very little flexibility and dictate to children, "Use the paper only in the correct way, do it the way you are told, stay in the lines." If you make use of them, understand their limited purpose: coloring within the lines and tracing patterns are small motor control exercises.

> Coloring books and teacher-prepared patterns and worksheets have absolutely nothing to do with fostering original thought and creativity, and in fact, by their very nature tend to squelch them.

ASK YOURSELF:

Do you limit the use of worksheets and patterns because they can inhibit a child's creativity?

81. When doing art projects, provide a generous supply of materials

BUNNIES WITH MEASLES

In the spring we made rabbit puppets. I then encouraged the children to create their own stories and puppet shows with the finished product.

I busily pre-cut the proper materials before the children arrived. For a group of eight children I would make 16 pink ears, 16 black dots for eyes, eight sets of whiskers, and eight strips of red to represent tongues when the mouths of the puppets were opened.

I'll never forget the last time I did this project that way. One of my students, a self-assured fellow named Doug, had just come back to school after being ill for two weeks. Doug rarely approached the art activity, but of course making a puppet had a little bit of extra allure to it, and he sat right down at the table. He then gathered up all the black dots and pasted them on the face of his puppet. He smiled broadly and said, "My rabbit has the measles." In the blink of an eye, all of my "eyes" for the other children had been used up. Of course, the other children wanted their puppets to have measles. I grabbed my scissors and quickly started cutting black dots. Then another child took the whiskers and said, "My puppet has hair." In addition to cutting extra black dots, I was now frantically trying to cut more whiskers to keep up with another unexpected demand. One assertive adult statement like, "Those dots are only for the eyes," or "That is not for hair but should be used as whiskers" would have solved my problem. But that would surely have stifled the children's creativity as well.

HELP!

The natural tendency is to say to the children, "The black dots are for the eyes," and give each child two dots. This is fine if you are teaching the fact that a rabbit has two eyes. However, for a creative experience where the children bring a little of themselves to the project, we should not impose our idea of what a rabbit puppet should or should not look like. More important, we need to recognize that we limit creativity when we provide limited materials.

When you do an art project, do not try to ration the supplies to any set number. If your goal is to encourage children to think for themselves, then do not try to predetermine what the finished product will look like by controlling and limiting materials. After all, the bunny with measles was a good idea.

ASK YOURSELF:

Do you recognize that when you limit the quantity of materials for art activities you may be squelching the children's imagination and forcing them to make what you think should be made?

Does the children's finished artwork all look the same, as though the children were trying to make something correctly or copy a model that you provided?

When you decorate bulletin boards with the children's artwork do you select only things that were done correctly, or do you value and display new and original ways to make things?

82. Value the process more than the product

SALLY SCISSORS

If it was rest time you could count on finding Sally, the teacher of the toddlers, sitting on the floor busy as a beaver cutting out shapes. You could almost tell what month it was by what Sally was busy cutting. She did it ALL—from leaves and acorns in September to the cows and lambs of May. This took a great deal of time and energy, but Sally was a very dedicated teacher.

During free play Sally would put out paint or Magic Markers and have the children decorate the leaf, cow, or whatever the pattern of the day was. I asked her if she thought all this cutting of paper patterns made a difference to the children and how they responded to the art activity. She thought a moment and said, "I don't really know if it matters to the children," and then added as an afterthought, "The parents seem to like it when they make something recognizable."

I challenged her to just put out a plain square piece of paper for the children to decorate to see if they responded differently. Sally tried this. She noted that the children were as enthusiastic as ever, and spent about as much time (we all know how quick that can be for a two-year-old) as they had in the past with the carefully cut out patterns.

Since Sally had such a talent for art, I encouraged her to spend some of her newfound spare time (since she could take a rest from cutting patterns) creating other longer lasting materials for the classroom, such as wall decorations or flannel board stories and songs. We both agreed that shapes on occasion would still be appropriate to provide some variety for the children and to keep their parents happy.

HELP!

Art activities for the young child should focus on the experience of using materials rather than on making a finished product. If you watch children very closely during an art activity, you will notice that half the time they are not even looking at what they are doing. They will look at someone else in the room or carry on a conversation with a friend—all while spreading the paint, glue, or whatever it is we have given them to use.

Usually we provide a Q-tip or paint brush, but given enough time and freedom, the children will want to dig right in and deal with the materials with their bare hands, and a few enthusiasts will go in right up to their elbows. When left undisturbed, children will usually choose to keep working the materials until they wind up with a gray or brown blotch on a piece of paper that is starting to shred from being overworked.

> Art for the young child is really a sensory experience. If we accept this, art projects become much easier to plan for. We still need to prepare and think, but the thinking is now different. Instead of what will they make, it becomes what will they EXPERIENCE as they interact with the materials that we provide for them to use.

ASK YOURSELF:

Do you treat art activities as exploratory experiences?

Do you value the process or the finished product?

83. Resist the temptation to label a child's artwork

WHAT ARE YOU MAKING?

Ramon had been painting at the easel for about three minutes, when Mrs. Hurry walked by. She became very excited at what Ramon had painted, saying, "Look Ramon, you made a bird, we need to save this." Without the slightest bit of hesitation, she removed the paper from the easel and put it on the drying rack. Poor Ramon, while he was delighted with the praise and attention he had received, I don't believe he thought he was done painting. He then shrugged his shoulders, put the brush down, and scooted off to the block corner.

HELP!

The child should be the one to decide when a painting is finished. The adult can suggest saving it and starting another painting, but doing that should be the artist's decision alone.

Occasionally a child under five will, by design or accident, create a recognizable object; however, we should resist the temptation to label what they are making or to ask them to identify what they have made. We need to remember that at this age, when it comes to artwork, young children are explorers, not producers. If you would like to stimulate conversation you can talk about color selection and brush stroke, or just ask one of the best all-purpose open-ended questions of all time: "Would you like to tell me about it?"

ASK YOURSELF:

Do you stop children before they are really done exploring with the materials?

Do you avoid labeling or identifying the children's creations?

84. Be aware of how you can inadvertently inhibit children's creativity

WHEN NOT TO BE AN EXAMPLE

I think play dough is great. I use it at least once a week. When circumstances allow (all children involved productively in activities) I like to sit down at the play dough table and join in. I tend to create and roll balls. The children usually notice what I am doing and pretty soon everyone is making meatballs. As a matter of fact, if I had planned a lesson on making meatballs, I would probably get the same results. Quite unintentionally, I have gained control of the activity. And therein lies the danger!

HELP!

We teach even when we don't plan to. An adult is a powerful and constant role model. (A heavy burden to bear.) For example, when we sit and doodle with a crayon, many children feel the need to try to copy what we have drawn. This can be frustrating for them since their skill level cannot match ours, and it is certainly stifling their creativity. If we truly want to foster children's creativity we must carefully limit what we do.

Deal with this challenge by avoiding being an example, or by providing several alternatives to the children. Now when I sit down with play dough, in addition to meatballs I make snakes, pizza, and other things. More important, I call everyone's attention to the different things each child is making. This helps to reinforce the value of different ideas and approaches.

The same attitude should hold true when making masks or whatever. If you feel you must, you can show a few examples of a finished product to help stimulate interest. But then your artwork should be put away, out of sight, so that the children are encouraged to think through making their very own creations.

Quite often with play dough, teachers unthinkingly put out materials that influence the children. Plastic cookie cutters, forks, knives, and spoons say "make food." Play dough should be put out by itself. To help the children explore the possibilities of the play dough material, you can occasionally add rollers, hammers, and items such as small cars, plastic blocks, pipe cleaners, potato mashers, pinecones, and anything else you can think of to add a new dimension. Please store the cookie cutters deep in the closet.

ASK YOURSELF:

Do you notice when children try to emulate what you have done?

Do you quickly put any teacher-made art examples out of sight so they do not become role models for the children to copy?

85. Accept the child's artistic interpretation

THE SKY IS BLUE

Five-year-old Christine had been working for a long time at the easel painting what appeared to be a flower. Miss Direction, her teacher, walked by. When Christine dipped the brush into the bright yellow paint and started to paint the top of the paper, Miss Direction said, "Oh no, Christine, the sky is blue."

HELP!

When a child paints a sky using yellow, dark colors, or perhaps a mixture of green and orange, it does not mean that she does not know the color of the sky. Do not assume that children need our guidance to show them the one right way to paint the sky, a tree, or anything else. Instead of trying to teach children to paint realistic pictures, we should encourage them to use their imagination and creativity.

We should view mixing colors as a creative expression of the child, accept it, and encourage more exploration and experimentation. Think of the paintings by Monet, Picasso, Van Gogh, or the illustrations in children's books by Leo Lionni or Ezra Jack Keats. They do not represent the sky with a blue stripe across the top of the page, nor should we ask children to. I think we need to be careful about our rush to correct and teach when it comes to the artwork of young children.

> Display inexpensive copies of artwork from different cultures and by famous artists such as Mary Cassatt, Wassily Kandinsky, Alejandro Xul Solar, Romare Bearden, and others, right alongside prints of Humpty Dumpty and other nursery rhyme favorites.

Every child is an artist. The problem is how to remain an artist once he grows up.

—Pablo Picasso

ASK YOURSELF:

Do you accept the children's experimentation with color and form, or do you try to get the children to conform and see the world the "right" way?

86. Provide art experiences in different locations

A FRESH PERSPECTIVE

As I walked past the four-year-old class I was surprised by how unusually quiet it was. When I peeked through the glass panel on the door, I saw only three children. I knew it was not their time to be on the playground and decided to see what was going on. Once inside I spotted the remaining children. They were all under the tables! Lying flat on their backs and with crayons in hand, they were drawing on paper that had been secured to the bottom of the tables. It brought to mind Michelangelo's painting the ceiling of the Sistine Chapel. Children who normally avoided art projects like the plague were waiting patiently for a chance to try this new perspective.

HELP!

All too often we think of art only at a table or easel, and usually on a piece of paper that is 9 by 12 inches. How refreshing it is for the children to work in a different location or position. For variety, hang large pieces of mural paper out in the hallway, or spread them across the floor and do open, cooperative projects. The children will just love having a great expanse of paper to work on. Painting or working on any large surface, such as a box or mural, will stimulate creativity.

> Don't forget about the playground. Occasionally do art activities there as well, such as letting the children use chalk on the blacktop or work at the easel.

ASK YOURSELF:

Do you provide art experiences in different locations, including on the playground, or is art always done at the art table?

Do you encourage the children to do cooperative art projects such as decorating large sheets of paper, big boxes, or other items?

87. Provide an environment that fosters creativity

CREATIVITY VERSUS CHAOS

I finished my college courses in December and needed a job. One of my instructors told me that there was a teaching position open in a nearby school. The current teacher of the four-year-old class was leaving in January. I thought this was a good possibility. After successfully completing the interview process, I learned about the downside. The director told me that she was sure there was nothing wrong with the children. She even went to the trouble to have a consulting psychologist, who had observed the class, contact me to repeat the fact that the children were normal. I started to become worried about what I was getting into. I needed the job and agreed to go visit the class. I observed for a morning.

During free play, there was an art activity that the children ignored. Three children in the housekeeping area were throwing dishes toward the book corner. Four children were involved in a heated chase game—get the bad guy—that circled through all areas of the room. One young man spent his time atop a stack of four blocks shouting loudly, "Batman"—a popular TV show at the time. The only calm, safe area seemed to be a corner where two easels were side by side. Dennis and Kevin were painting. After a few minutes, Dennis turned to face Kevin. Dennis used his brush to paint Kevin's arm and then his chest (They were in smocks). Kevin looked at Dennis and decided to join in this new game. They proceeded to paint one another!

On the playground, I asked the teacher what she thought of the class. She replied that the children were just fine, but the parents could not understand her total commitment to creativity.

Desperate for a job, few to be found that time of year, I accepted the challenge. It turns out the teacher was half-right; the children were fine. However, I think the parents were also correct. A strong commitment to creativity does not mean allowing anarchy. There need to be some rules and expectations about behavior. The teacher has a responsibility to provide a safe and pleasant environment for all the children.

HELP!

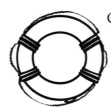

Creativity does not mean chaos. When trying to decide whether or not to try an activity, I have found it helpful to go through a basic list of four questions:

1. Will this activity pose a safety hazard to anyone?
2. Will this activity destroy or damage property?
3. Will this activity intrude on the privacy, rights, or activities of others?
4. Will this activity show disrespect of others' beliefs?

If the answer to all of the above is NO, then and only then, I say, "Why not?" and give it a try. Remember, just because you try something does not mean you are committed to stick with it or have to repeat it. We can always change our mind and say that it did not work. On the other hand, think of all the wonderful discoveries you may have in store with a carefully considered philosophy of WHY NOT?

ASK YOURSELF:

Do you create an environment that fosters creativity without being chaotic?

Do you teach children to respect others and their ideas?

Try This

Collect thought-provoking pictures for the children to look at and discuss.

Try the popular pastime of looking at clouds and imagining seeing different shapes.

Use paint to create inkblot pictures for the children to look at and discuss.

Create a dramatic play prop box. Include props that suggest vacations, such as things we use at the beach, on a picnic, or when camping.

Provide materials for the children to do 3-D art work:
- ☆ Aluminum foil
- ☆ Paper that can be folded, curled, or twisted
- ☆ Egg cartons, baskets, boxes, or Styrofoam trays that can be decorated with toothpicks, straws, tongue depressors, ribbon, or cotton balls

Paint or make prints with unusual items:
- ☆ Feather
- ☆ Straw
- ☆ Lego blocks
- ☆ Cut-up pieces of old flip flops
- ☆ Twigs
- ☆ Potato masher

Use more than paint and plain white paper at the easel. Try painting on newspaper, colored paper, or corrugated cardboard. Provide chalk, pencils, pens, crayons, and Magic Markers.

Play a music tape while children are doing art work. Vary the musical selections to suggest different moods. Play different kinds of music, such as classical, jazz, and country.

Have the children make a smell collage.

March to a Different Drummer

Using Music and Creative Movement to Enhance Children's Learning

Music is much more than a good way to calm the children before naptime, keep the group busy while others are in the bathroom, or transition to the next activity. It is a powerful teaching tool and should be a regularly planned part of the daily routine. Concepts, such as big/small, high/low, loud/soft, fast/slow; directional words such as up/down, over/under, front/back; sequencing; and recognition of colors, numbers, and letters can all be taught through musical activities and finger plays.

We do not have to teach children to like music; that comes naturally. This is the ideal time to help children explore the many different kinds of music the world has to offer. Whether you are doing creative movement, playing instruments, or just listening to a tape at naptime, don't limit yourself to only standard children's music.

Music is a pleasure and should be enjoyed everyday, not just when the music specialist comes to visit.

Music is the universal language of mankind.

—Henry Wadsworth Longfellow

179

88. Use background music sparingly

TOO MUCH OF A GOOD THING

Music in elevators, music while on hold on the telephone, and music in the stores at the mall, I feel, is overkill. We live in a very noisy society. We use noise to cover noise, the same way we use an air freshener to cover a bad odor.

Some teachers play background music in their classrooms. I don't really think anyone is paying attention to it (any more than in the elevator), but it is there. This can have a negative impact. While it is arguably true that the music will drown out some of the noise from down the hall, it also causes people to have to talk a little louder in order to be heard over the music. Playing background music can cause the sound level in a classroom to get uncomfortably loud.

HELP!

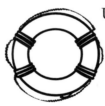

Use tapes and CDs sparingly. Trying to use them for atmosphere can cause the noise level to become loud and uncomfortable, defeating their intended purpose. Quiet or a normal classroom hum is not a bad thing.

ASK YOURSELF:

Do you use tapes or CDs in an attempt to cover or mask noise?

Do you find yourself talking louder than normal to overcome the sound of the music?

89. Be willing to sing

YOU COULDN'T CARRY
A TUNE IF I PUT IT IN A BUCKET

When I was a young child, I was told, "You couldn't carry a tune if I put it in a bucket." In the third grade I tried out for the school glee club. The very tactful music director said she really needed an announcer more than another singer. Another blow to my ego came when I took the oral exam for my children's music course in college. One requirement was to be able to sing three songs picked at random from the curriculum. When I had finished, the very considerate instructor lovingly put her arm around my shoulder and said, "You'll use the piano a lot." I nodded my head and got a passing grade for the course. My piano skills were minimal, I could hardly play anything using both hands, but what else could she say?

When I taught my first class, in spite of my checkered past, I decided I should at least try to sing. I was literally amazed when I overheard the children on the playground singing the songs I had introduced to them on key and with the right melody. I don't know how they did it with me as the role model, but they did!

HELP!

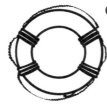

Children enjoy hearing an adult sing. They don't care what your skill level is. You do not have to sing like Diana Ross. Just close the door to the room for a little privacy, and then sing, sing, sing! You and the children will be happier as a result.

Use what talent you possess: The woods would be very silent if no birds sang except those that sang best.

—Henry Van Dyke

ASK YOURSELF:

Do you sing in the classroom?

Do you rely too heavily on tapes, CDs, and records?

90. Use singing and creative movement to make transitions easier

SING YOUR WAY THROUGH THE DAY

An experienced elementary school teacher was preparing to teach a two-year-old group for the first time. She expressed some concerns about how to get the children to gather for story time. I suggested that when she wanted to get the children's attention she should just start singing. While initially embarrassed at the prospect of singing in public, she reasoned that no one was likely to listen anyway, and so she decided to give it a try. Much to her delight, when she began singing the children stopped their activities and gathered around her. From that point on I could hear her singing often during the course of the day.

HELP!

Many teachers tend to call out instructions when they want to gather everyone together to leave the playground, line up to go down the hall, or change actvities. (Adults usually are not aware of how much unnecessary yelling/shouting they do.) Some teachers use bells or whistles to get the children's attention; singing is much nicer.

Singing can be used very effectively to draw children to an adult or an activity. We all have cleanup songs, why not a "Go in from the playground" tune, or "Let's march down the hall" song. Children quickly join in a song, and you will find you have to do a lot less shouting when you do a little more singing. Sing your way through the day. It makes for a much more pleasant atmosphere.

Use moving from point A to point B with the children as an opportunity for fun and creative movement. There is no reason why we can't be butterflies, jump, or walk sideways, backwards, or bent over on our way to the bathroom, playground, or wherever. Sometimes let the children select the mode of movement. I find I have better control and attention when we move in a special way, as opposed to the traditional single line. Occasionally, for a change of pace, walk in a line since that is a necessary skill for the children to develop.

The children will move in orderly lines for many years in the future. Let's take advantage of the understanding atmosphere of a preschool to foster creative movement.

Where words fail, music speaks.

—Hans Christian Anderson

ASK YOURSELF:

Do you use music and creative movement to make transitions easier and more pleasant for you and the children?

Do you encourage creative movement throughout the day?

91. Select simple songs to teach the children

SINGING SOLO

One of the loneliest and most difficult things I do is to sing solo when I introduce a brand new song to the children. They cannot read the words and will learn the song only by hearing it sung over and over again. If I am lucky, by the third time I sing it, some of the children will join in, at least on the chorus. For this reason I introduce only one or two new songs a week.

HELP!

Since you must sing solo until the children learn the song, choose your material very carefully. Songs that are long and have complicated verses are a poor choice. If you as the adult need a cue card to help you remember the words, then it's a sure sign that it will be too difficult for young children to learn easily. Songs that are repetitive and have a simple chorus work best. Try to incorporate some sort of hand movement or gestures to keep those who have not yet learned the words actively involved.

> Make nursery rhyme songs, lullabies, and simple folk songs part of your repertoire.

ASK YOURSELF:

Do you choose developmentally appropriate material for the children to sing so they can readily join in, or do you sing songs to the children while they sit passively and listen?

92. Create original songs

A HAIRCUT SONG

James brought a frog to class. To honor the occasion I sang the
popular song "Five Speckled Frogs." When I finished singing
Leon said, "I got a haircut, sing a song for me." Unlike for frogs,
I really did not know any classic tunes about haircuts.
I had to improvise and create a haircut song.

HELP!

Children just love listening to songs about
themselves, their activities, or their treasured possessions.
Creating your own songs for special events is not that hard
to do. Use a simple familiar tune (let's not make this too
complicated) like "Mary Had a Little Lamb" or "Hot Cross
Buns" and put in your own words. For example:

Tune: Mary Had a Little Lamb

Leon had his haircut, haircut, haircut
Leon had his haircut
And he looks very handsome

Maria found a pretty leaf, pretty leaf, pretty leaf
Maria found a pretty leaf
And she named it Lily

Bill's grandpa is coming, grandpa is coming, grandpa is coming
Bill's grandpa is coming
And they are going to the movies

If you sing along as you read my examples, you will notice that not all the
lyrics match the rhythm of "Mary Had a Little Lamb." You should try your
best to keep a steady rhythm, but please don't let worries about rhyming or
perfect rhythm stop you from the fun of creating your own songs; create
whatever songs you want.

When you create original songs, the children will catch on pretty quickly and soon will be creating songs of their own. Some of their songs may become class favorites.

ASK YOURSELF:

Do you try to personalize songs, or create songs to honor special events?

Are children encouraged to create original songs?

93. Use musical activities and finger plays to teach sequence and letter recognition

WHY GO ON A BEAR HUNT?

One of the most popular activities in a preschool classroom is "Let's go on a bear [sometimes lion] hunt." It is always a lot of fun, and the children enjoy participating. But too many teachers rush through this gem and miss the great learning potential that it has to offer. In addition to the fun of the hand activities and the sounds we can imitate as we slush through mud or creep through tall grass, there is an underlying lesson of sequence—on the way to the cave, and then in reverse order when running home to safety.

To enhance the learning experience you can change the order, as well as lengthen or shorten the sequence to fit the group you are working with. While doing the part where we run back to safety you should ask the children, "What comes next?" "Where do we go?" "What do we do?" With the excitement of the bear chasing us, this then becomes a great lesson in recall and sequencing.

HELP!

Music lessons can do much more than entertain. When doing finger plays and songs, we should think about what the children can learn from the activity. Is there the potential to teach numbers, letters, or other basic concepts? Keeping it entertaining is very important, but we should recognize and take advantage of the learning potential in musical activities.

The great classic song "Bingo" can be modified to help children recognize letters, learn to spell, and read their names. Replace the name Bingo with a child's name, for example, "There was a boy who had a dog and Jason was his name—O." To take this a step farther and make it a reading experience, prepare index cards with all the children's names printed on them. As you hold up each card, the children's first challenge is to recognize whose name is printed on it. The fun starts when you sing the names and corresponding letters (J-A-S-O-N) instead of B-I-N-G-O. Obviously names like Jason and Grace will work better than Al and Jennifer, but sing all the names modifying the rhythm as needed. The children can learn not just how to spell Bingo and their own names, but also to recognize and spell most of their classmates' names as well.

Songs and finger plays can be used to teach opposites, such as fast/slow, front/back, up/down, big/small, or over/under.

ASK YOURSELF:

Do you use musical activities and finger plays as teaching tools?

94. Use props to encourage creative movement

GIVE THEM SOMETHING TO HOLD ON TO

I was conducting a workshop on music and movement for a group of Georgia Head Start teachers. To get everyone in a creative mood, I put on some ballet music and asked the assembled group to pretend to be snowflakes. I got a lot of "Do we have to" comments and several blank stares. Finally, some very cooperative souls, sympathetic to my plight, did a few twirls. The lesson was a disaster. Of course, asking a group of adults from Georgia to be snowflakes was not the brightest idea to begin with.

The next time I tried a similar activity, I asked the teachers to pretend to be leaves in the wind, and I gave them crepe paper streamers. The streamers made a world of difference in their attitude. Making the paper swirl and twirl was readily accepted, no blank stares or nervous giggles—now they had a mission they readily understood.

HELP!

While adults have more inhibitions about creative movement and pretending than children, the use of props is a good idea at any age. Scarves, hoops, magic wands, fairy dust, sheets, balls, and streamers can be used to stimulate creative movement. The children will get so focused on moving the props that they relax and their body movement flows naturally. Eventually, after several successful creative movement experiences, they can move on to activities without the support of props.

One of the best activities I have found to stimulate creative movement is to let the children suggest how to move. To get started, I show one way to move your hands, such as shaking them. I then ask if they know any special ways to move their hands. You can also ask the children to move just their feet, one hand and one foot, face, or their whole body. Inviting each child to show his special way of moving is a great way to encourage individuality and creativity. If you use music during this activity, you will find that varying the tempos will influence the children's movement.

ASK YOURSELF:

Do you limit music lessons to singing songs, or are there opportunities for creative movement as well?

Do you provide materials to promote creative movement such as scarves, feathers, hoops, and balls?

95. Minimize the use of commercially produced activity tapes

MARCH TO YOUR OWN BEAT

Activity CDs and tapes always sound great when I first hear them. Often I will screen them at home or perhaps while driving to work. It is quiet, there are no distractions, and I think to myself, "This will be great!" Like so many things, the theory (or the way it looks in the catalog) is better than the reality.

There are inherent problems associated with using activity tapes. Children usually find it difficult to hear and/or understand the instructions. There are always parts that seem too short and others that seem to go on forever. Let's face it: These are mass-produced, one-size-fits-all activity records. Each group of children is different, and we should do our best to tailor the material to meet their needs.

HELP!

You can get all sorts of ideas from tapes and CDs; however, when it comes time to have music with the children, try to use music that you can control. Put on some lively music with a steady beat, or slow music (depending on what the activity is) and then just call out the instructions. This way you can control the pace of the activity, vary it as needed, and as an added bonus, invite the children to make suggestions on what to do.

A simple drum beat, chanting, or clapping of the hands to keep rhythm also works nicely. When you clap the rhythm, you are in total control, not someone that recorded the music in a studio a thousand miles away. I am not advocating tossing out your collection of CDs, tapes, and records; rather, consider this as a way to individualize and expand the materials you use.

> Don't hesitate to create your own tapes.

As with all materials, music should be previewed before being used with the children. Be sure you are not choosing selections that are too loud or dramatic for the young child.

ASK YOURSELF:

Do you use commercially produced music activity tapes that limit your ability to be responsive to the children?

Do you create your own music tapes, play an instrument, or bang out rhythms on a drum so you can modify the lesson to fit the needs of your class?

96. When doing creative movement, encourage children to come up with their own interpretations

PLEASE DON'T BE AN ELEPHANT

In the spring, some teachers do units on the circus. During this time of year, when I observe music lessons, I am almost sure to see an adult bent over at the waist, arms extended and hands clasped together, moving in a slow plodding fashion— obviously an adult interpretation of an elephant (or perhaps someone with back pain).

HELP!

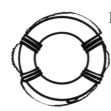

In music, as in art, we should try to stimulate and inspire the children's imagination, but this cannot be accomplished by providing examples or models. Modeling in essence says to the child, "Look at me; this is how it is done."

A good example of how carefully children watch and copy an adult comes from my very early years as a teacher. I always joined in the movement activities with the children. One of their favorites was a jumping song. (It was a good aerobic workout.) When I was seven months pregnant I still wanted to participate and decided to modify my jumping. I kept my feet on the ground but moved the rest of my body as though I were jumping. (Sort of modified deep knee bends.) Some of the children noticed and started jumping like they were seven months pregnant too.

> Teachers are powerful role models even when they aren't trying to be. There is a huge difference between joining an activity and dominating it. When trying to foster creativity we must be careful to recognize the difference and act accordingly.

Children do not create in a vacuum, and we do need to stimulate their minds before asking them to participate in creative movement. Before asking a child to move like an elephant, we should provide some pictures and encourage discussion. How big is an elephant, how does it move, how does it eat, what does it sound like, if you were an elephant what would you do? Ask the children to think about the subject. Only after doing that should you have them pretend to be elephants.

> When children are exploring with movement, try to compliment different interpretations. Recognizing the various ways children are moving their bodies will encourage them to stretch their imagination and be even more creative.

ASK YOURSELF:

Do you stifle creativity by showing children the correct way to be a lion, elephant, or any other animal or thing?

Do you guard against becoming a role model when doing creative movement with the children?

Do you use pictures and/or discussions as a way to stimulate the children's imagination before asking them to do creative movement?

97. Do not limit creative movement to a circle pattern

DO YOU ALWAYS GO IN CIRCLES?

When I observe a class doing a movement activity, such as pretending to be giraffes or horses, they always seem to be going in circles. For safety reasons this pattern makes a lot of sense. However, do we always have to do it this way? Snowflakes moving in circles?

HELP!

 Creative movement should not always have to be done in circles. It reminds me of having to stay inside the lines of a picture in a coloring book. Not very creative! When doing any activity that involves movement there need to be some rules for safety. Children should be reminded that bumping, crashing, or falling down (unless we are doing leaves in the fall) is not acceptable because someone could get hurt.

We need to remember that on the playground, children exhibit great skill at avoiding crashes when running or riding tricycles. They have this same skill indoors, and can usually manage to move safely in a less restrictive pattern than the traditional circle. We know which children may need a little extra guidance, and sometimes having only half the group move at a time is a good idea. (Be sure the seated children have something to do, like playing rhythm instruments. Telling them to sit still and just watch the other children move is asking for problems.) We do not always have to move free of a circle pattern, but we should not always have to be IN a circle pattern.

ASK YOURSELF:

Do you overcontrol creative movement by always requiring children to move in a circle, thereby defeating its very purpose?

98. Control the pace of creative movement activities

LIONS, TIGERS, AND BEARS

Miss Take was almost in tears. She had just finished teaching a creative movement lesson where the children were pretending to be lions. The children had become very stimulated, got overenthusiastic, and the lesson ended in chaos. She was vowing either never to do creative movement again, or in the future to restrict the children to being butterflies or caterpillars.

HELP!

Creative movement is a wonderful activity, and if properly planned for, need not be feared. In the wintertime, when energy levels are high and playground time is short, the opportunity for children to pretend to be lions, tigers, or bears can be very useful. We just need to have a game plan to keep things from getting out of hand. For example, you could control the pace of the activity by having a picture, toy, puppet, or surprise bag handy that you know the children will want to see. This works like a magnet to attract them after the movement. Another approach is to pre-select the order, plan on being snakes or butterflies after lions or tigers. I usually end as birds, and fly the flock to the next activity.

ASK YOURSELF:

Do you pace the children when doing creative movement, allowing them to be very energetic, and then in a positive way calming them down again?

99. Vary the use of musical instruments

BE MORE THAN A MARCHING BAND

James Levine (referred to as "his smilingness" by co-workers) is the music director of the Metropolitan Opera in New York City. When he is on the podium conducting the orchestra he puts his entire body and soul into the performance. Watching his arms move and his body sway is like watching a ballet. He certainly makes it look like being the conductor of a large orchestra would be great fun.

HELP!

Musical instruments are not just for marching bands. With four-year-old children you can be a bit more sophisticated. Create your own orchestra. Have the children with triangles, bells, and shakers sit on the left side, those with tone blocks, drums, tambourines, and cymbals on the right side, and rhythm sticks in the middle. (Any arrangement would do.) Put a few large blocks together to create an official podium for the conductor. Then establish a few hand signals. For instance, when the conductor points at your section you can play, when she holds her palm up it means stop playing, and we all should try to match the speed of the baton, playing slowly when it is moved slowly, or fast when it is moved quickly.

Initially you should be the conductor, but once everyone understands the ground rules turn the baton (usually an odd rhythm stick) over to a child to lead the orchestra. What fun, what power and control. This activity provides a great opportunity to emphasize following directions and cooperation.

The children can play their instruments with or without recorded music. If you do use recorded music be sure to vary it. Use everything from Mozart and Miles Davis to John Philip Sousa marches.

A shortage of drums or any prized instrument can present problems. Ask the children to switch instruments with one another frequently to ensure that all of the children get to play several instruments, including the drum. Of course you can make your own drums out of oatmeal or coffee containers. Don't hesitate to have just a drum band.

Provide musical instruments so the children can explore different sounds. These should be available throughout the day, not just at music time.

ASK YOURSELF:

Do you use musical instruments often and in different ways?

Are musical instruments available for the children to play throughout the day, or are they available only during adult-supervised music lessons?

Try This

Visit or have someone come to you from:
- ☆ A dance studio
- ☆ Musical instrument store
- ☆ High school band
- ☆ Local community orchestra
- ☆ Glee club or choral group

Create your own musical instruments:
- ☆ Make a rubber band guitar by stretching a few rubber bands of differing widths across a box
- ☆ Make shakers and rattles; put different things in them

Have the children experiment with sounds that they can make using their body. For example, hum, clap hands, slap leg, stamp feet.

Play games like Freeze: Have children walk, run, slide, or move in creative ways to music; when you stop the music they have to freeze in position.

Put on music and have the children pretend to be ice skating.

Have the children make props for creative movement. Attach ribbons or crepe paper streamers to paper plates or tongue depressors.

Use a varying drum beat to encourage the use of large muscles. When developmentally appropriate, ask the children to roll on the floor, jump, run, go forward or backward, twist, gallop, or skip.

Encourage creative movement by using tape to mark off special zones on the floor, for example, hot zones, fast zones, or tired zones.

Have children pretend to be a balloon. They can expand, float, and go flat.

Have children use creative movement to explore scientific concepts:
- ☆ Life cycle of a butterfly—caterpillar, cocoon, butterfly
- ☆ Actions of bees—when worker bees discover pollen they fly back to the hive and do a dance to communicate the location of the pollen

Have children listen to music and then create a story about it.

Accompany readings of poetry with rhythm instruments.

Afterword

If you have classroom stories, ideas, or suggestions that you would like to share, I would love to hear from you. Please e-mail them to me at gwenkaltman@hotmail.com. Be sure to include your name, so that you can be acknowledged if your material is included in a future publication. Thank you for sharing!

Resources

Help Yourself: Creating Your Own Plan for Improvement

The best way I know to ensure continued growth throughout your career is to try new things and develop the ability to honestly evaluate your own work. In those areas that you determine you can do better, reread the chapter and then use the form on the next page to plan your strategy for improvement. I urge you to take your time. Please do not rush quickly through the book. You are trying to develop new skills, and in some instances a change in attitude that will become a part of who you are. This takes time and consistent effort.

As you develop the skill to analyze your own work—no simple feat—you will be creating a powerful tool for self-improvement. When you do your self-evaluation, remember to consider not only what went wrong but also what went right. Be sure you note the date on your form and keep it as a reference for future years. I suggest that you repeat this process every year, as you are sure to change and evolve.

If your initial attempts do not work as well as you had hoped, do not be discouraged. What is important is that you are learning about yourself and developing your skills as a teacher. Children are pretty resilient. If an activity or approach does not work out quite the way you envisioned it, the children will survive the experience and so will you!

No one knows what he is able to do until he tries.

—Publilius Syrus

Improvement Plan

Date: Chapter:

Ask yourself:

My plan for improvement:

_____

My initial observation (evaluate the children's response):

My second observation (if applicable):

<u>Reflections:</u>
Based on your observation(s), what part of your plan worked well?

How would you modify it in the future?

What other ideas or strategies could you try?

Helpful Organizations

Association for Childhood Education International
17904 Georgia Avenue, Suite 215
Olney, MD 20832
(301) 570-2111
http://www.acei.org

Child Care Information Exchange
PO Box 3249
Redmond, WA 98073
(800) 221-2864
http://www.ccie.com

Child Development Associate
Council for Professional Recognition
2460 16th Street, NW
Washington, DC 20009
(800) 424-4310
http://www.cdacouncil.org

Clearinghouse on Early Education and Parenting
University of Illinois at Urbana–Champaign
Children's Research Center
51 Gerty Drive
Champaign, IL 61820
(217) 333-1386
http://ceep.crc.uiuc.edu

Head Start Information and Publication Center
Head Start Bureau
Administration for Children and Families
U.S. Department of Health and Human Services
1133 15th Street, NW, Suite 450
Washington, DC 20005
(866) 763-6481
http://www.headstartinfo.org

National Association for the Education of Young Children
1509 16th Street, NW
Washington, DC 20036
(800) 424-2460
http://www.naeyc.org

National Association for Family Child Care
5202 Pinemont Drive
Salt Lake City, UT 84123
(801) 269-9338
http://www.nafcc.org

National Association of Child Care Professionals
PO Box 90723
Austin, TX 78709
(800) 537-1118
http://www.naccp.org

National Child Care Information Center
Child Care Bureau
Administration for Children and Families
U.S. Department of Health and Human Services
243 Church Street, NW, Second Floor
Vienna, VA 22180
(800) 616-2242
http://nccic.org

National Network for Child Care
Cooperative State Research, Education, and Extension Service
U.S. Department of Agriculture
1400 Independence Avenue, SW
Washington, DC 20250
(202) 720-7441
http://www.nncc.org

Southern Early Childhood Association
PO Box 59930
Little Rock, AR 72215
(800) 305-7322
http://www.southernearlychildhood.org

Zero to Three
National Center for Infants, Toddlers and Families
2000 M Street, NW, Suite 200
Washington, DC 20036
(202) 638-1144
http://www.zerotothree.org

Suggested Reading

Barbour, A., & Desjean-Perotta, B. (2002). *Prop box play: 50 themes to inspire dramatic play*. Beltsville, MD: Gryphon House.

Bredekamp, S., & Rosegrant, T. (Eds.). (1992). *Reaching potentials: Vol. 1. Appropriate curriculum and assessment for young children*. Washington, DC: National Association for the Education of Young Children.

Bredekamp, S., & Rosegrant, T. (Eds.). (1995). *Reaching potentials: Vol. 2. Transforming early childhood curriculum and assessment*. Washington, DC: National Association for the Education of Young Children.

Copley, J. V. (Ed.). (2004). *Showcasing mathematics for the young child: Activities for three-, four-, and five-year-olds*. Reston, VA: National Council of Teachers of Mathematics.

Coughlin, P. A., Hansen, K. A., Heller, D., Kaufmann, R. K., Stolberg, J. R., & Walsh, K. B. (1997). *Creating child-centered classrooms: 3-5 year olds*. Washington, DC: Children's Resources International.

Dodge, D. T., Colker, L. J., & Heroman, C. (2002). *The creative curriculum for preschool* (4th ed.). Washington, DC: Teaching Strategies.

Eliason, C. F., & Jenkins, L. T. (2003). *A practical guide to early childhood curriculum* (7th ed.). Upper Saddle River, NJ: Prentice Hall.

Feldman, J. (2000). *Transition tips and tricks for teachers*. Beltsville, MD: Gryphon House.

Harlan, J. D., & Rivkin, M. S. (2004). *Science experiences for the early childhood years: An integrative affective approach* (8th ed.). Upper Saddle River, NJ: Prentice Hall.

Helm, J. H., & Katz, L. (2001). *Young investigators: The project approach in the early years*. New York: Teachers College Press.

Hendrick, J. (2001). *The whole child: Developmental education for the early years* (7th ed.). Upper Saddle River, NJ: Prentice Hall.

Isbell, R., & Raines, S. C. (2000). *Tell it again! 2: Easy to tell stories with activities for young children*. Beltsville, MD: Gryphon House.

Jones, E., & Nimmo, J. (1994). *Emergent curriculum*. Washington, DC: National Association for the Education of Young Children.

Mayesky, M. (2002). *Creative activities for young children* (7th ed.). Albany, NY: Delmar.

Owocki, G. (1999). *Literacy through play*. Portsmouth, NH: Heinemann.

Raines, S. C., & Isbell, R. (1999). *Tell it again! Easy to tell stories with activities for young children*. Beltsville, MD: Gryphon House.

Schiller, P. (2001). *Creating readers*. Beltsville, MD: Gryphon House.

Seefeldt, C. (2005). *Social studies for the preschool/primary child* (7th ed.). Upper Saddle River, NJ: Prentice Hall.

**CORWIN
PRESS**

The Corwin Press logo—a raven striding across an open book—represents the union of courage and learning. Corwin Press is committed to improving education for all learners by publishing books and other professional development resources for those serving the field of PreK–12 education. By providing practical, hands-on materials, Corwin Press continues to carry out the promise of its motto: **"Helping Educators Do Their Work Better."**